TRAILS WEST

WHITTLESEY HOUSE

McGraw-Hill Book Company, Inc.

NEW YORK   TORONTO   LONDON

TRAILS WEST

AND

MEN WHO MADE THEM

EDITH DORIAN
&
W. N. WILSON

CONTENTS

Often ox power was not enough, and panting men with bulging muscles struggled to move a wagon a few miles a day.

IN THE BEGINNING

No matter where you are when you pick up this book—down east in Maine, midwest in Iowa, far south in Florida, on the Pacific Coast in California—you can walk out of your front door and find a road. It may be a winding, shady, unpaved country lane; it may be a noisy, bustling city street, but it is a road. And if you walk around a corner, you come to other roads stretching away into the distance. But a little over 300 years ago when the first English children opened their front doors in Plymouth, they were lucky if they found even a footpath running past their houses toward the common where the settlers pastured their cows.

When your family wants to take a trip, your father stops in a filling station and asks for a road map so he can learn the best roads to follow to reach any place you want to go anywhere in the whole United States. But when the early settlers wanted to go somewhere, there were no road maps to consult, no highways to follow, nothing except the narrow trails the Indians had worn—down to the shore to fish and dig clams; deep into the forests to hunt game; through the fields to gather blackberries and blueberries in season; off to the north to spend hot summer months on cool lakes and salty bays—trails for everyday living and for warpaths against their enemies.

And since there were no other roads to use, white men also followed the Indian trails when they hunted food for their families or explored the new land. At first they followed them afoot like the red men; later they chopped them out to widen them for wheeled carts and horses. For, as more towns grew up in the new country, farmers wanted to cart their produce to barter for "store" goods like tea and sugar, merchants had to stock their shelves with the supplies English ships brought into harbor towns like Boston, or militiamen and soldiers had to rush help to village after village when the Indians took up the hatchet against the white man.

Americans these days take superhighways and dual-road parkways for granted and they would certainly turn up their noses in disgust if they had to jolt over the ruts and holes and through the mud of any of the early roads in the English colonies along the Atlantic seaboard. The colonists themselves sometimes turned up their own noses when carriage wheels mired deep in mud or axles snapped on rocks and potholes! Travel was slow and hazardous; it took three weeks, instead of five hours, to journey by road from Boston to New York. But travel the colonists had to and travel they did to transact business, to settle in new towns, to visit relatives in other colonies north or south, sometimes even just to see the sights of the big towns like Philadelphia and New York.

Of course, by the time of the Revolution, minor roads fanned out in all directions from town to town, and major post roads linked all the colonies together. From our point of view they were not very good roads, but over them went the traffic of their day: post riders with the mails, elegant private carriages belonging to the rich merchants of the North and the prosperous planters of the South, lumbering wagons filled with freight or farm produce, peddlers on horseback with their wares, heavy stages carrying ten or twelve passengers, messengers on fast horses rushing communications from the Congress in Philadelphia to General Washington or to patriot leaders in every colony.

But beyond the mountains westward of the seaboard, the Blue Ridge, the Great Smokies, the Alleghenies, the Cumberlands, in the vast lands that were to become great states in a new republic, there were still no roads in the white man's sense of the word, only the age-old buffalo traces and the trails of the nomadic red people.

12

And in the whole exciting story of the thirteen British colonies that grew up to be a mighty, independent nation stretching from ocean to ocean across a great continent, nothing is more exciting than the story of the famous trails by which America moved west.

In your whole life you may never come closer to the Mississippi or the Rockies or the Texas rangelands than New York City, but the opening of our West is as much a part of your heritage as if you had been born within a stone's throw of the old Oregon Trail. The story of Coronado and Father Kino, of Père Marquette and the Sieur de la Salle, of Mountain Men like Jim Bridger and Tom Fitzpatrick, of fighting Cheyennes and fierce Dacotah Sioux, of scouts like Kit Carson and Daniel Boone, of frontier marshals like Wild Bill Hickok and Wyatt Earp, of traders like the Bents and Jesse Chisholm, of emigrant wagon trains forted up against Kiowas or Blackfeet, of explorers like Lewis and Clark, of cowhands trail-ing Longhorns, is your story in a very real sense. Their courage and endurance, their restless, adventurous spirit, their long hunts and lonely wanderings helped to shape us into Americans. Words like roping, claim-jumping, stogies, barbecues, cowpunchers, bull-whackers, mule skinners, and chuckwagons sometimes bewilder our foreign visitors, but they don't bewilder us. Shout "come and get it" and Americans within hearing won't stop to ask what they are to come and get. They'll come and bring their appetites with them! For the terms of the old trails color our speech today just as they did a hundred years ago when the West was young.

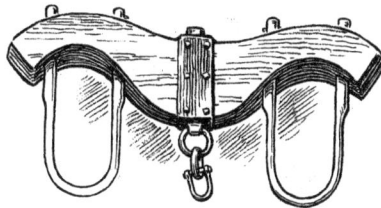

A two-storied, mud-colored Zuñi pueblo whose defiant Indian defenders flung rocks down upon the heads of the Spaniards.

THE GOLDEN TRAIL

In any account of America's trailmakers — after the buffalo and the Indian — the Spaniards come first, mapping the way for later pathfinders. Where they expected to find cities of gold, they found mud-colored pueblos and piñon nuts, desert and cactus, prairies and blizzards, but they crossed North America from Galveston to San Diego; from Sonora to Santa Fe; from the west coast of Mexico to Monterey.

But the Spaniards did not think of themselves primarily as colonists and trail blazers. Columbus had found "the birthplace of gold!" And because he had taken possession of the New World in the names of King Ferdinand and Queen Isabella, the adventurers came hard on his heels. They had not come to chart the New World. They had come to make their fortunes. Cortés spoke for them all when he first haughtily refused grants of land in the West Indies. "But I came to find gold," he retorted, "not to till the soil like a peasant."

Practically all of these men were looking for something fabulous that did not exist, a Fountain of Youth or an El Dorado. What most of them found instead was infinitely more valuable than the stored treasure of any Indian ruler — the vast fertile lands and the rich natural resources of an unexplored continent. But few of these early adventurers could grasp that idea. They came from a country impoverished by centuries of warfare, and their minds focused only on gold. In the New World, men told each other, Indians stored gold the way Spanish farmers stored grain. Even

15

Records and maps made by Franciscan
and Dominican friars who shared the
Spaniards' dangers in the New World still
preserve the story of those first explorers.

if a man left home a poor nobody, he could soon have fame and
fortune — and return to a castle in Spain! So the Spanish conquest
began, the first American gold rush, the most audacious, cruel,
greedy, and tireless of any America has known.

Nowadays it is easy to smile at the dream of a Fountain of
Youth in Florida, of Seven Golden Cities in New Mexico, and of
the Kansas kingdom of Quivira where everyone ate from golden
plates. But in the sixteenth century the fortunes men actually made
in the New World were nearly as incredible as those dreams. The
treasurer of Santo Domingo grew so rich he put gold dust in his
salt shakers at a banquet! After being gone only two months,
Alonso Niño and Cristóbal Guerra sailed home to Spain to stride
ashore "loaded with Venezuelan pearls as though they were hay."
And Cortés lined his own pockets, as well as the king's, with the
golden nuggets and the jewels he seized from the conquered Aztec
ruler, Montezuma of Mexico. There was no telling what a man
might find if he hunted hard enough; other Mexicos might still lie
hidden a little farther north in the wilderness. New Spain, the
empire Cortés had created for the rulers of Castile from his con-

16

quest of Mexico, was fine. But loading your own purse with gold and silver and turquoise was finer!

Consequently, the Spaniards rode hot-spurred on their golden trail into Texas, into New Mexico and Arizona, into Kansas, even across the desert into California. They found the Grand Canyon of the Colorado; they discovered the Zuñi and Hopi pueblos; Acoma, "the city on a rock"; they saw the vast bison herds on the prairies. In fact, the "roads" which their narratives say they followed north were the roads made by those shaggy migratory herds on yearly trips between summer and winter feeding grounds.

For actually the "pathless wilderness" of the Spaniards was not a pathless wilderness at all; it was penetrated in every direction by thousands of trails linking together all parts of what is now the United States. They were Indian trails, of course, but many of them had originally been made by the buffalo. Indeed, buffalo roads played a vital role in the story of America. Used first by the red men, they were followed next by the earliest white explorers, then by soldiers, scouts, and trappers, later by settlers, and later yet by highways and railroads. Even now we still drive along roads first chosen by the Spaniards' "humpbacked oxen," and cross bridges built where their thundering hoofs used to splash through shallow fords.

Chasing rabbits helped to make Wichita
Indian boys fleet-footed.

From the headwaters of the Potomac to Florida, from Pennsylvania to New Mexico and across the Great Plains, the hoofs of 60,000,000 bison trampled out America's first "roads."

What manner of men were these adventurers that history calls Conquistadores — conquerors — who came into our West and Southwest seeking gold? Before they invaded the New World many of them had fought in Flanders and laid siege to the Moors. Warfare was no new story to them. They were hardy men, lovers of danger, gamblers willing to stake their heads on a possible fortune. They were superstitious, greedy, and cruel. They worked the conquered Indians till they dropped. To teach them a lesson, Coronado burned not half a dozen, but 200 Indians simultaneously at the stake before he rode on in his gold-plated armor to seek his mythical kingdoms of gold. Small wonder that when he came back again, he found his garrisons massacred and the pueblos aflame with hatred of the Spaniards.

But there was another side to the Conquistadores. If they were ruthless, they were also courageous, proud, energetic, and daring. The southern sun turned their steel armor into ovens that seared their backs, but it could not stop them. Nor could rivers, deserts, mountains, and Indians. They were never more than a handful

18

among the tribes they encountered, but thanks to two assets, horses and superior weapons, they fought and struggled successfully through the wilderness, painfully learning the deadly accuracy of an arrow in the hands of an Apache and the disastrous folly of loading pack mules with fancy clothes and silver candlesticks instead of extra food.

De Soto, "the inland Columbus of Florida," who found the Mississippi; Coronado whose expedition discovered the Grand Canyon and the Hopi pueblos and crossed the Arkansas into Kansas; Cabrillo, who explored the coast of California, and Father Serra, who labored to establish its missions; Oñate, who colonized New Mexico; Father Kino, who began the settlement of southern Arizona and charted the Colorado; de Anza, who blazed the way across the California desert more than half a century before covered wagons rolled over the United States to the West Coast — all made American history.

Today three of our states — California, Colorado, and Nevada — still bear Spanish names. Literally dozens of our rivers and mountains and hundreds of our towns are known by the names of saints dear to those long-ago Spaniards. Even now, from Los Angeles to San Antonio, their language is spoken by upward of two million Americans, vigorous testimony to the impact of the sandaled friars and the steel-clad soldiers from Spain.

Spanish soldiers carried matchlock guns whose priming had to be ignited by a slow-burning match.

Watchful scouts warned their villages of
La Salle's coming well ahead of his arrival.
News traveled quickly among the Indians.
In fact, relays of fast runners could carry
an important message several hundred miles
in a single day.

THE WATER TRAIL

Unlike the Spaniards, the pioneers of France in the New World did not come seeking Golden Cities or the treasures of Indian rulers. The merchants, adventurers, and fishermen sailing from the ports of Brittany and Normandy under the Lilies of France hunted less glittering riches: codfish, furs, and the ivory tusks of walruses. Breton fishermen claimed the discovery of the chilly shores of Newfoundland and found its waters teeming with fish. Early explorers, working their way into the St. Lawrence, noted the possibilities of a valuable trade in furs. At least two French ships a day were sailing for the cod banks during the winter of 1545, and in 1578, 150 of the fishing vessels off Newfoundland belonged to Frenchmen who combined cod-catching with lively trading for bear and beaver skins among the Indians.

In the eyes of Spain, of course, both the French and the English, who were also nosing about the Atlantic Coast, were foreign intruders. In spite of the Breton fishers' claims, in spite of the voyages of Jacques Cartier into the St. Lawrence and of John Cabot's explorations for England, Spain acknowledged no claim to any part of North America except her own and Portugal's. In fact, in 1541 when His Most Catholic Majesty of Spain discovered that His Most Christian Majesty of France had actually authorized Jacques Cartier and Sieur de Roberval to establish a colony in the New World, he speedily invited Portugal to join in an expedition against the encroaching French. But Portugal failed to see what harm a few Frenchmen could do in the cold and distant land

21

Cartier and the Breton fishermen had discovered. The expedition did not materialize, and the French calmly continued their plans.

Cartier and Roberval's attempts at colonization collapsed, and a small settlement made at Port Royal on the Bay of Fundy in 1605 fared no better, but French enterprise was not daunted. Another group set out under the leadership of stouthearted Samuel de Champlain, who had been at Port Royal, and this time they were successful. In 1608, on the site of the Indian village of Stadaconé, which Cartier had visited nearly seventy-five years earlier, Champlain founded New France. That first colony is now the Lower Town of old French Quebec. By 1634 Champlain had also established Trois Rivières (Three Rivers) at the mouth of the St. Maurice River where its three channels enter the St. Lawrence, and in 1642 a band of priests, nuns, and settlers under the guidance of Sieur de Maisonneuve founded Ville Marie de Montréal. Like Quebec, Montreal occupies the site of an Indian village visited by Cartier in 1535, though both villages had vanished before Champlain's arrival. The Indians had called their palisaded town on its island in the St. Lawrence Hochelaga, but Cartier, climbing and christening Mont Réal (Mount Royal) behind it, had found a name for a French settlement a hundred years before it was founded!

The real pioneers of our American West were now ready to begin their task. For the fur-trading French, following a water route, penetrated the continent westward to the Rockies and southward to the Gulf of Mexico, establishing a chain of trading forts and missions in their wake. Though great seigneuries developed from land grants to men of rank or of special service to their king, the lords of those vast, self-sufficient estates were often as concerned as the thrifty merchants of the new towns in the profits to be made from furs. Explorers, voyageurs, and *coureurs de bois* (woods runners) ranged far and wide seeking new sources of supply, and missionaries, intent on the salvation of the Indians, accompanied them or followed hard on their heels.

22

Naturally, since the interests of the fur trade were opposed to the spread of population and settlement which would drive game before them, the colonies in New France grew slowly. Champlain had his hands full trying to strengthen Quebec and keep peace among its quarreling inhabitants, at each other's throats over fur profits. But he still found time to listen to stories poured into his ears by fur-bartering Indians, of fertile lands and beautiful lakes. In fact, he even found time to see Lake Oneida, Lake Champlain, and Lake Huron for himself.

Unluckily for the fortunes of New France, however, he saw them in the company of Montagnais and Huron Indians on expeditions against their ancient enemies the Iroquois — one reason why Americans say "good morning" instead of "*bon jour!*" The powerful Confederacy never forgave the French. Montreal, Three Rivers, and Quebec lived in terror of the Mohawk war whoop, and all during the long contest of France and England for America, the Iroquois Confederacy fought relentlessly on the side of the English.

Beavers played a major role in the exploration of the West, for the value of their pelts lured trappers deeper and deeper into the wilderness.

Champlain was the "father of New France," but others followed him. Patient, daring, and indomitible men, their names now star the map of a nation no one had dreamed of when they were burying iron disks marked with the claims of France beside our inland waterways. Stephen Brulé traveled along Lake Huron to find rich copper mines in the country beyond, to see Lake Superior and the strait we call Sault Ste. Marie. Jean Nicolet paddled to the tip of Lake Huron, along the Straits of Mackinac into Lake Michigan, and then explored the Wisconsin River. Pierre Radisson and Sieur des Grosseilliers returned to Montreal with an escort of 300 Plains Indians and sixty canoes loaded with bison, beaver, and sable skins to set every fur trader in New France planning to find the lands not just farther west but southward as well. Louis Joliet and Father Marquette found the waters that flow through those lands: the Fox, the Wisconsin, the Mississippi, the Illinois, the Ohio, the Missouri and the Arkansas, portaging at the site of modern Portage, Wisconsin, and of modern Chicago.

Sieur de La Salle, whose path crossed Marquette's at Sault Ste. Marie and Joliet's near Lake Ontario, built Fort Frontenac on that lake in modern St. Lawrence County, New York, sailed the first trade vessel across the Great Lakes from Lake Erie to Lake Superior, raised his string of forts down the Mississippi Valley — Fort Miami at the mouth of the St. Joseph River, Fort Crevecoeur on Lake Peoria, Fort St. Louis on the Mississippi — and journeyed through the Illinois into the Mississippi and down to the Gulf of Mexico to name and claim Louisiana, the entire Mississippi Valley, for his king. Henri de Tonti of the Iron Hand, La Salle's faithful friend and lieutenant, showed himself able to accomplish more with only one hand of flesh and blood than most men with two! Du Lhut, Tonti's cousin, the great *coureur de bois*, visited the Mille Lacs Lake in Minnesota, exploring and trading throughout the Lake Superior region where Duluth still hears his name.

And the Vérendryes, father and four sons, like Joliet born in New France, with far-flung fur interests, built trading forts on

Rainy Lake, the Lake of the Woods, the Red River, and the Assiniboine River; and voyaged down the Assiniboine to the Missouri to visit the Mandan villages in 1739 — the same villages where two great American explorers, Lewis and Clark, would winter more than half a century later. Two of the Vérendryes, their courage unshaken by the death of their oldest brother at the hands of Sioux, found their way into the Black Hills of modern South Dakota and Wyoming, burying their iron plate for France near Pierre (South Dakota) where American school children would find it sticking out of the ground in 1913!

It had taken 150 years, and it had been an arduous task, but the Water Trail was open — with only short portages — from Labrador, down to the Gulf of Mexico. For France her intrepid sons laid claim to the heart of America, lands watered by great rivers, ranged by warlike tribes, roamed by "huge beasts with horns and hoofs and curly hides." But in the process they helped create the story of a nation yet to come, the United States of America.

The difficulty of poling back against the mighty currents of the "Father of Waters" made flatboat trade on the Mississippi and Ohio a one-way business.

Having to stop and clear fallen trees out of the road frequently added days to the long, hard journey into Kentucky. The best marksmen were the lucky ones: they stayed on guard while the rest chopped!

THE WILDERNESS ROAD

Nowadays a motorist can still ride through the Cumberland Gap into Kentucky, the "dark and bloody ground" of American history, over Daniel Boone's Wilderness Road, for since 1926 many miles of the old Trail have been incorporated in a section of U.S. 25, the popular Dixie Highway. In fact, if the driver chooses to turn off at Mount Vernon, Kentucky, he can find Crab Orchard, Danville, and Bardstown, towns that Daniel Boone knew, too. And though no trace of Daniel's famous Boonesborough now remains, except a marker, the modern traveler on Kentucky's Highway 35 can stop in Pioneer Memorial State Park and prowl around restored Fort Harrod, originally built in 1774, a year before Boone began chopping out the Wilderness Road.

Unlike the adventurous, fur-trading French of Canada, the English along the Atlantic seaboard let a hundred years pass before they began their first western settlements. Most of them had come to the New World to build permanent homes for themselves and their children's children after them, and they were soon too busy with the practical problems of daily living to bother with the uncertainties "back of beyond." Besides, though the French had that almost continuous waterway from the St. Lawrence to New Orleans, hundreds of miles of mountain wall lay between the English colonies and the Ohio, their first navigable river west.

Nevertheless, by their original far-reaching land grants, some of the English colonies claimed large tracts beyond the Allegheny Mountains, and though her indignation had no effect, Virginia protested vigorously when the French built Fort Duquesne at the Forks of the Ohio where Pittsburgh now stands. The French and Indian War was about to begin — the last war in the long struggle between the two great European powers for the possession of North America. It would end with the British Union Jack flying over what had formerly been New France.

Signs of serious trouble were everywhere, and in the Valley of Virginia the Indians were growing increasingly sullen and treacherous under the influence of the French. At night in lonely cabins along the frontier, people were rousing to the fearful peal of the war whoop, and hunters passing clearings were finding scalped and mangled bodies in charred ruins. By 1754 war had started in earnest, and the next year General Braddock marched out of England's new Fort Cumberland on the Potomac in Maryland to drive the French and Indians at Fort Duquesne back to Canada. Everyone knows that he actually marched to meet death in a ravine at Turtle Creek, only a few miles from the fort he had come to capture. Not everyone realizes that among the survivors of that massacre there were *two* young men, not just one, destined to make American history — Daniel Boone, the young backwoodsman from the Yadkin Valley in North Carolina, as well as George Washington, the young colonel from Virginia.

Daniel Boone was under twenty-one then, but his skill as a scout and his knowledge of Indian tactics might have been put to better use than driving a wagon. For he was a born woodsman. Even at thirteen he had served ably as chief scout and hunter for a caravan of settlers, his own family among them, migrating from Pennsylvania to the Yadkin. Plodding along, bored, in the rear of Braddock's slow-moving army, he had listened interestedly to the tales of the trader John Finley about a no man's land called Kentucky. Lying beyond the mountains, it was a safe home for no tribe, but a hunting ground for dozens. Buffalo in countless herds wearing paths to its salt licks, deer, otter, bear, wild turkey — its game made it sound like paradise to a backwoodsman whose

There was wild celebration in their villages when a Shawnee war party captured Daniel Boone, but the wily scout proved slippery to hold.

gun had to provide food. Someday soon, Boone decided, he would seek Kentucky for himself.

But it was not until the spring of 1769, fourteen years after he had served with Braddock, that Daniel Boone finally followed the Indian trail through the Cumberland Gap into Kentucky. That hunting trip lasted nearly two years. He was separated from his wife and children. He had his first unpleasant taste of Indian captivity. His beloved brother-in-law disappeared without a trace — though five years later, on a hunting trip, Daniel finally found a few bleached bones and a powder horn with John Stuart's initials on it in a hollow sycamore trunk. When his brother returned to the Yadkin for supplies, he was alone and in constant danger for months on end. Twice the Indians captured all the furs accumu-

29

lated to pay for outfitting the trip — and still Kentucky was all Daniel Boone had dreamed it would be!

So after two more exploring trips, he was again scouting for a caravan of settlers, and this one was heading for the Cumberland Gap. But Kentucky still proved hard to reach. Another Indian war halted the little group of settlers in Powell's Valley on the Tennessee side of the Gap, and the men had to turn to fighting instead of building a new town in Daniel's "Promised Land." When that war was over, however, there was no man along the border better known for cool courage and wily skill as an Indian fighter than Daniel Boone.

Back in the settlements, the story of his daring trip into Kentucky with his friend Michael Stoner, to cover 800 miles in sixty days and rescue surveying parties from massacre, lost nothing in the telling. Judge Richard Henderson of North Carolina, full of his scheme to organize the Transylvania Company and make his fortune settling Kentucky, eagerly sought out Boone. Henderson wanted two things: he wanted the Cherokees rounded up so he

Restored blockhouse at old Fort Harrod in Pioneer Memorial State Park, Kentucky.

could buy their claim to Kentucky, and he wanted a road. He got both. Daniel gathered the Cherokees together at a place called Sycamore Shoals, and on March 10, 1775, he began the Wilderness Road. All unknowing, Daniel Boone had started his career as history maker, for his road was to become a new nation's highway of empire in the first peopling of the West.

Naturally, Boone's road-building crew of "thirty guns" was made up of backwoods Indian fighters, not of modern engineers with bulldozers and steam shovels. So, if they managed to avoid the steepest descents and the worst climbs, blaze the trees, and cut the undergrowth back far enough not to choke their road in summer, they were satisfied. Naturally, too, they preferred their scalps on their heads instead of hanging at the belts of a Shawnee war party! Scouts were constantly active, and though some of the men were wounded, they succeeded in preventing serious surprise attacks. Following an old buffalo trace and Indian path, Boone and his men hewed their road over the mountains and into Kentucky until they could cross Rockcastle Creek. Then, instead of continuing westward, where they could have used an Indian trail to the Forks of the Ohio, they headed for what is now the heart of the Blue Grass region. The site Boone had chosen for the first Transylvania settlement lay near the junction of the Kentucky River and Otter Creek. Consequently, the road builders hacked and chopped and burned the rest of the way mile after slow mile.

Interestingly enough, the Indian trail they had followed through the Cumberland Gap and for 50 miles on the Kentucky side was one of the greatest of them all. Athiamiowee, Path of the Arméd Ones, the Indians called it. Beginning at Sandusky Bay on Lake Erie, the Warriors' Path ran south through the center of Ohio to cross Kentucky near modern Winchester and head for the Gap where it joined a northern trail, the Great Indian Warpath, which went into upstate New York by way of two prongs through Pennsylvania. Daniel Boone, hacking white civilization's first highway through the mountains, was already writing the beginning of the

31

last chapter for the Warriors' Path. His road spelled doom for the shadowy, fantastically painted figures who had moved silently along it in a hundred years of warfare between the powerful Iroquois Confederacy of the north and the warrior Cherokee of the southern hills.

But in 1775 the final words of the chapter were not yet written, and for seven years of war, Boone had cause to remember the grim warning of a Cherokee chieftain at Sycamore Shoals: "Brother, it is a good land we sell you, but you will find it hard to hold." They found it "hard to hold." Through much of the Revolution the fate of the Kentucky settlements seemed certain destruction. Panic-stricken fugitives hurried to the three largest stations or fled back to the seaboard. Virginia had her hands too full to send much help to the West, and, urged on by the British at Detroit, the Indians swore to wipe out every white and burn every cabin. In 1777 not even strong parties of settlers dared move about Kentucky. Harrodsburg was besieged three times and Boonesborough twice. Contact with the outside world came practically to an end.

Yet those dark days produced men and women whose names still stir America with pride: Simon Kenton, the lighthearted young blond giant with iron nerves, eavesdropping from Indian camp to Indian camp to bring warning of new dangers to the settlers; thirteen-year-old Jemima Boone and her two friends, captured by Shawnees, keeping their wits, stumbling and falling again and again to leave a surreptitious trail of torn clothing for Daniel and his rescue party to follow; Nolichucky Jack Sevier, later governor of Tennessee, carrying guerilla warfare to the Cherokee villages; Jemima Sugget Johnson, gambling on the chance that the hidden Indians still thought they could surprise the garrison, leading its twenty-eight heroic women and girls outside the palisades for the water without which Bryan's Station could not stand siege; George Rogers Clark, with only seven borderers, getting ammunition through from Virginia to Boone and winning unbelievable victories at Kaskaskia and Vincennes; Boone himself, escaping from his Indian captors, racing on foot from Chillicothe, Ohio, to Boones-borough, Kentucky, in four days to save the settlement; Boone, the incredible, whose resourcefulness overcame every obstacle, whose courage and cheerfulness kept heart in the rest.

Even after the Revolution, however, travel by the Wilderness Road was still hazardous. It became usual to wait at specified places until a large enough group had gathered to make the chances of getting through alive more certain. "A large company," wrote the *Kentucky Gazette* in 1788, "will meet at the Crab Orchard the 19th of November in order to start through the Wilderness. As it is very dangerous on account of Indians, it is hoped each person will go well armed." Still, as far as Indian attack went, the Wilderness Road was never as dangerous as the easier water route down the Ohio and western emigrants continued to choose it — though it was what it had always been, the difficult, miry, narrow trail chopped out by Boone and his companions, full of twists and turns, holes, rocks, and loose boulders. Until 1796 it was not even passable for wagons, yet before that date, toting all they possessed on packhorses, 75,000 men, women, and children had already followed the Wilderness Road west.

The flintlock gun and a beaver trap.

Mile after weary mile, Andrew Jackson's soldiers hauled their cannon through the mud and mire of the Trace to win a smashing victory over the British at New Orleans. The War of 1812 was already over, but in those days of slow communication, neither army had heard that news!

NATCHEZ TRACE

Nothing could stop the westward march of America for long. Except in the blackest years of Indian attack, family after family braved incredible dangers to follow Daniel Boone's Wilderness Road into Kentucky, and by 1780 a group of pioneers led by James Robertson had pushed through Tennessee to hack out a clearing for a stockaded log garrison and a handful of cabins. That new settlement was Nashville, and for eighteen years it was the farthest, most isolated outpost on our frontier. Then, in 1798, by the terms of a treaty negotiated three years earlier, Spain formally turned over to the new United States the whole area known as the Natchez District. Two thousand square miles more territory had come under the protection of the Stars and Stripes, and the frontier had advanced all the way to the Mississippi!

But 500 miles of swamps, bogs, creeks, rivers, and tangled forests lay between Nashville on the Cumberland River and our new outpost, Natchez on the Mississippi — 500 miles almost completely uninhabited by Americans and running straight through the tribal lands of the Choctaw and Chickasaw Indians. Of course, the easiest route from Nashville to Natchez and the lower Mississippi Valley was by water down the Cumberland, Ohio, and Mississippi Rivers. But before the days of steamboats, getting back against the Mississippi currents was next to impossible. Obviously a road between the two towns was vital. Troops might have to be rushed to the defense of the new territory, and regular mail service had to be maintained. Besides, with trade growing between

35

Natchez and the settlements back in Tennessee and Kentucky, the whole frontier would be clamoring for a road.

Fortunately, there was at least a path to use, the old Indian trace running north from Natchez, the trace that early Tennessee records call Notchey because it was marked by blazed trees. These days travelers can ride along a fine new highway, the beautiful Natchez Trace Parkway, but underneath there still lies the unpaved, one-way wagon road that General Andrew Jackson and his men slogged through, hurrying to the defense of New Orleans in the War of 1812. That is, it still lies underneath except where modern engineering has enabled the Parkway to go straight and true instead of tying itself up into 18-mile loops like the old Trace to avoid deadly bogs! For in spite of the efforts of the army and of private contractors to keep the Natchez Trace passable for wagons, a good deal of the traffic over it had to be by foot or by horseback. Just when everything seemed under control, rain would turn a low spot into a hopeless swamp or a creek into a torrent.

After Andrew Jackson had taken his troops over the Trace to the rescue of New Orleans, then to fight the Creeks at Horseshoe Bend in 1814 and again to tackle the Florida Seminoles in 1818, he was quite ready to recommend building another easier and more direct road south. A military road to New Orleans was actually finished, but the southern route did not immediately supersede the western Trace — perhaps because the Postmaster General discovered that mail sent over that road often *never* got through!

And certainly it was lucky for travelers on the Natchez Trace in its earliest days that they were not as fussy as travelers today. Most of the time people simply built a fire to keep wild animals off, buried their money in a hole in the ground, and slept in the open with a gun under their arms. When the English naturalist Francis Baily went over the road in 1797, he had to pay twenty-five cents, a good stiff price in those days, to the inn at Grindstone Ford for a supper of mush and milk, and the privilege of sleeping on the floor in a room with thirty other travelers plus saddles, bridles,

36

baggage, and lumber! But except in some hospitable Chickasaw Indian towns, that inn, only 70 miles out of Natchez, was the last shelter he found on the whole length of the Trace until he was close to Nashville. When his provisions ran low, he had to live for three days on nothing but pulverized corn.

Somewhere around 1800, however, "stands" (inns) began to be established about every 20 miles along the 500 miles of the road, supposedly spaced so that United States postriders could reach one every night. Apparently it was a lot safer to sleep on the ground than among the cutthroats and dirt in some of them, but merchants and itinerant preachers using the Trace describe others as "fine public houses." The best of them, of course, advertised stables and blacksmith shops, as well as beds and meals, and kept supplies of bacon, biscuits, sugar, and coffee on sale for the long trip through the wilderness.

With outlaw gangs like Sam Mason's on the prowl, Trace travelers slept with a gun under their arm and one eye open.

In spite of floods, swamps, and outlaws, hard-riding post carriers somehow
got through with the U. S. mail.

In the Trace's heyday approximately twenty-five "stands"
flourished on the road, and a goodly number of them were kept by
Indians. Both the Choctaw and Chickasaw nations had finally
granted the United States the right to a "horse path" through their
tribal lands, but when it came to Americans' opening "houses of
entertainment" in their territory, they reared right back on their
haunches and balked! They did agree, however, to open "stands"
themselves and appoint "suitable" Indians to run them. What's
more, they ran good ones. David Folsom, the first of the Choctaw
chiefs to be elected by their new neighbor's democratic system of
ballots, ran the "stand" at Pigeon Roost, and James Colbert ran
the one near the old U.S. Chickasaw Indian Agency.

Like Folsom, James Colbert was half Indian and half white.
His mother was a Chickasaw and his father was a Scotch trader
who had been adopted into the tribe. And, again like Folsom, he
and his three brothers, William, Levi, and George, all became in-
fluential chieftains. George operated the Chickasaw ferry over the
Tennessee River, a very profitable undertaking, and Levi not only

38

shared an interest in that, but owned farms, salt springs, grist mills, and many slaves! Curiously enough, William Colbert's partner was a famous Indian fighter, John Gordon, first postmaster of Nashville and close friend of General Jackson, under whom he had served as "captain of mounted spies" in the Creek War. So where the Trace crossed the Duck River, the white ex-soldier and the powerful Chickasaw chief operated a ferry and owned a "stand" together on land granted Gordon for fighting Indians!

In fact, the history of Indian and American relations on the Natchez Trace is peaceful compared to the story of other trails. The Choctaws occasionally exacted "an eye for an eye and a tooth for a tooth" when white men killed a member of their nation, but the Chickasaws boasted that they had never spilled the blood of an Englishman or an American in anger. The old Trace, nevertheless, is still rich in memories of its Indian past. In 1729, when it was only an Indian trail, the little remnant of the great Natchez tribes had fled over it to take refuge with the Chickasaws 300 miles northward. Goaded beyond endurance by the terrible cruelty and injustice of a stupid French governor, they had risen in fury and wiped out Fort Rosalie and the French settlement flourishing on their own bluffs above the Mississippi. French Natchez never recovered from the blow, but soldiers from New France practically exterminated the Natchez Indians in retaliation.

Still, if any descendants of those survivors who fled along the Indian Trail were around later to help the Chickasaws lick a combined French and Choctaw force thoroughly and competently, their war whoops must have been the loudest in the fight! That battle was one of the most decisive in colonial American history, because it helped break French control of the Mississippi tribes. It all happened more than 200 years ago, but twentieth-century Americans can still see the battlefield preserved as Ackia Battleground National Monument at Tupelo, Mississippi, and visit the spectacular Indian mounds outside of Natchez, especially the Fatherland Mounds on the west bank of St. Catherine's Creek, which might possibly be the site of Tattooed Serpent's Grand Village those long-ago Frenchmen knew.

But if the Indians along the Trace were generally pleasant, the outlaws were not — and the Natchez Trace specialized in outlaws! Many a man disappeared for good journeying between Natchez and Nashville, and many an unidentified skeleton washed out of a shallow grave beside the road. People claimed that Sam Mason, the most dangerous and daring rascal of them all, posted spies at all the inns in Natchez to learn how much money prospective travelers on the Trace would have with them. Usually they had plenty; two or three thousand dollars in a man's moneybags was commonplace. Business was booming at Natchez, and homeward-bound merchants and traders carried their profits with them. In 1801 more than a million dollars worth of American merchandise went downstream to Spanish New Orleans, and in 1803, after Napoleon had decided he would rather have $15,000,000 for his war with England than the Louisiana Territory Spain had re-ceded to France, business boomed still more. For President Jefferson's diplomatic mission had made the Louisiana Purchase, and we owned New Orleans ourselves. Even as early as 1797, Francis Baily, the Englishman who did not like the inn at Grindstone Ford, said that the traders traveling with him were "much concerned" when an accident frightened their pack horses off in every direction. They had good reason to be "concerned." Some of those horses were loaded with nothing but dollars!

Even the "Kentucks," as people called the boatmen, generally broke up their flatboats when they sold their cargoes, sold the timber for firewood, and hoofed it home over the Trace. But since other travelers described them as sunburned and "dirty as Hotten-tots," and their clothes as "black, greasy and tattered," the "Ken-tucks" sound more likely to scare an outlaw than to tempt him! Besides, they had already celebrated pay day in town.

But the outlaw reign of terror got so bad that the army was ordered to put a detachment on the Trace, and the President offered a reward of $400 to anyone who captured a bandit. What happened? A couple of Mason's own men finally buried a tomahawk in their leader's brain and carted his head off to Washington, Mississippi, to claim the reward! Luckily, before they could collect they were recognized and speedily tossed into jail to await trial — and the gallows.

Even as old a hand in the wilderness as Meriwether Lewis found traveling the Natchez Trace more deadly than finding a trail to Oregon. Today a monument to his memory stands close to the site of Grinder's Inn, where the famous explorer met his death, quite probably by murder. Yet until 1830, the Trace was still called the "safest and surest" land route between Washington, D.C., and the lower Mississippi Valley!

Where the Trace wandered mile after mile through tribal lands, Choctaws and Chickasaws maintained both ferries and "stands" for travelers.

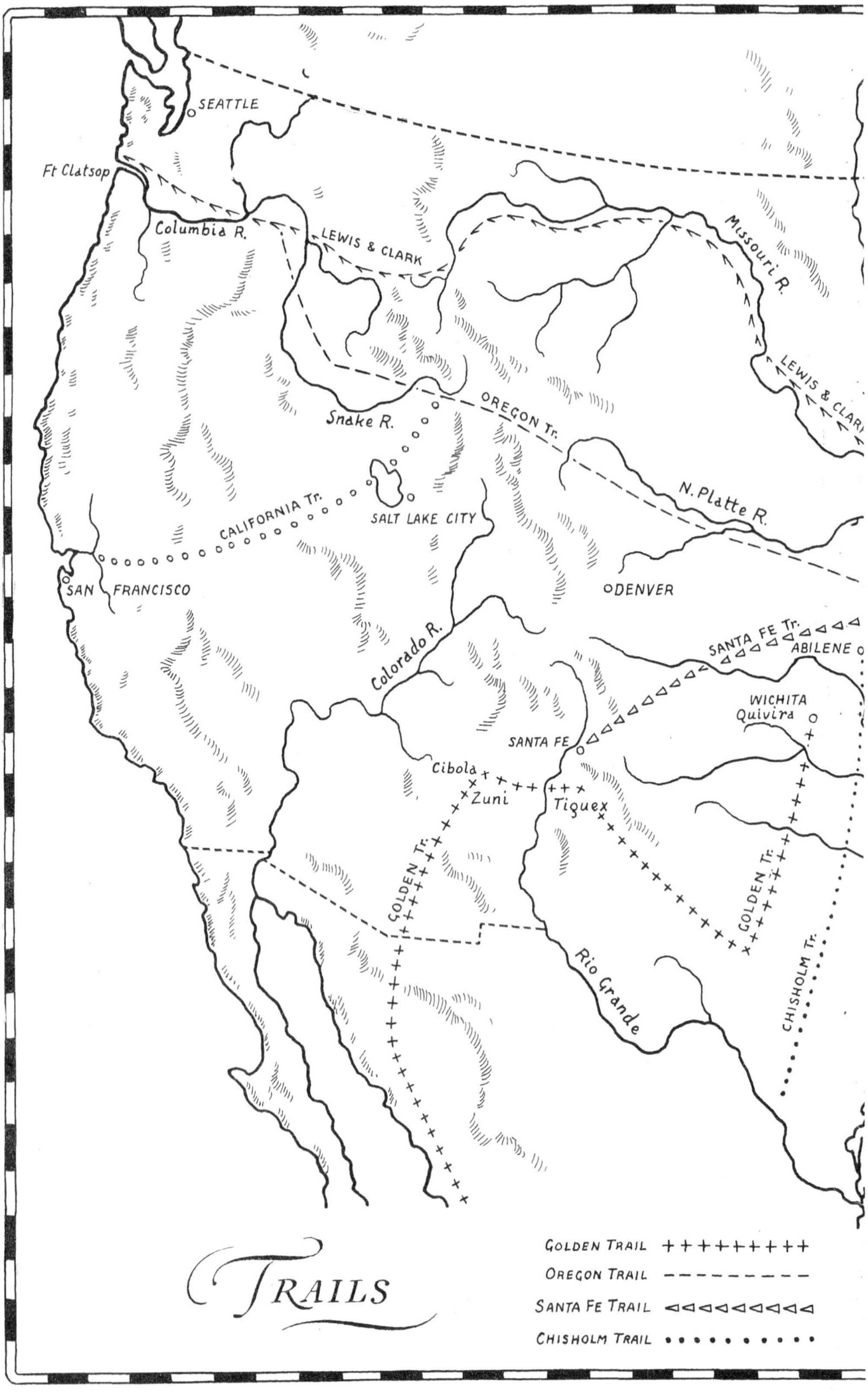

SEATTLE

Ft Clatsop

Columbia R.

LEWIS & CLARK

Missouri R.

LEWIS & CLARK

Snake R.

OREGON Tr.

N. Platte R.

CALIFORNIA Tr.

SALT LAKE CITY

SAN FRANCISCO

○DENVER

SANTA FE Tr. ◁ ◁ ◁

Colorado R.

ABILENE ○

WICHITA
Quivira ○

SANTA FE ○

Cibola +
×Zuni

Tiguex

GOLDEN Tr.

GOLDEN Tr.

CHISHOLM Tr.

Rio Grande

*T*RAILS

GOLDEN TRAIL + + + + + + + +
OREGON TRAIL − − − − − − − −
SANTA FE TRAIL ◁ ◁ ◁ ◁ ◁ ◁ ◁ ◁
CHISHOLM TRAIL • • • • • • • • • • •

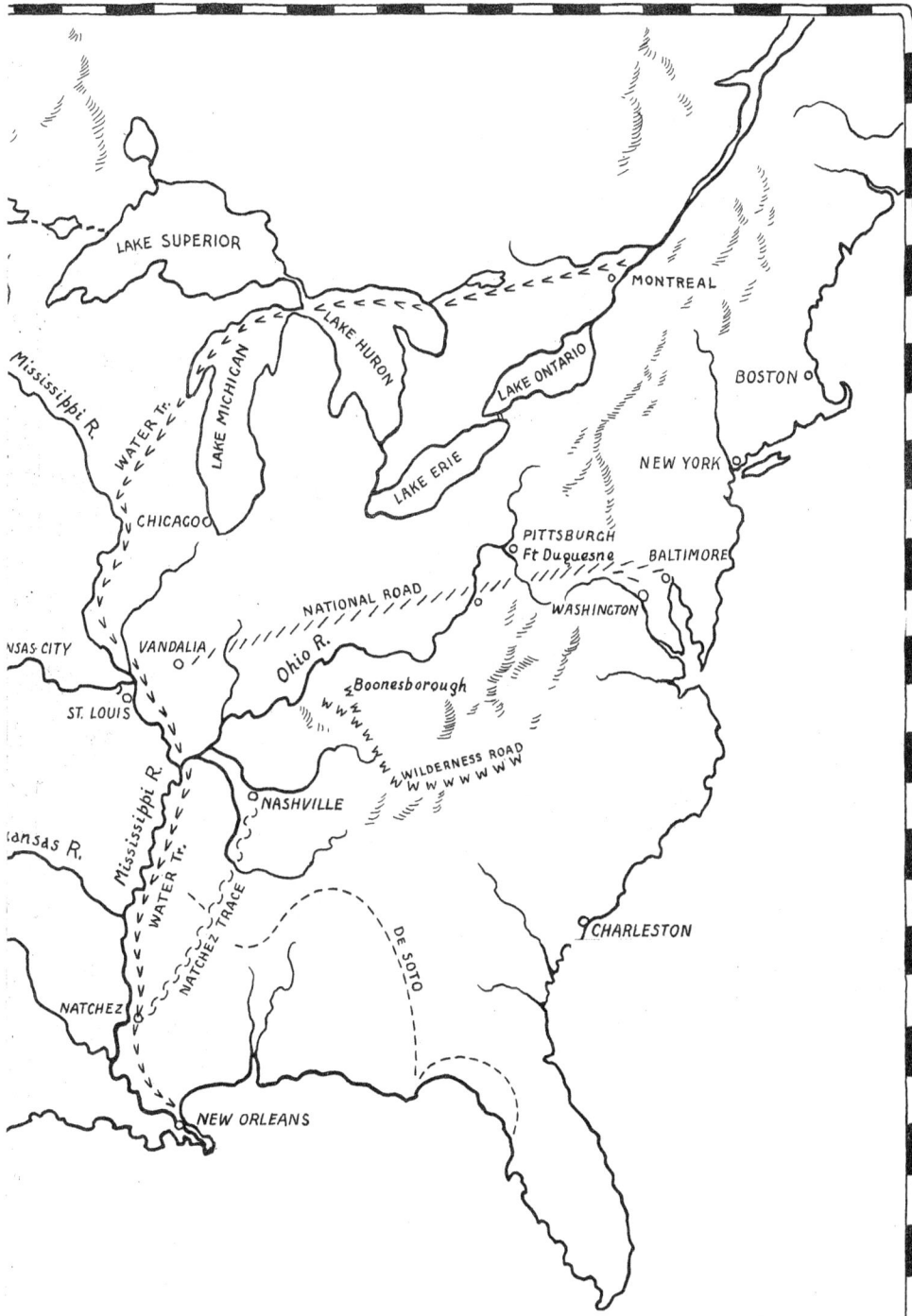

LAKE SUPERIOR

Mississippi R.

WATER Tr.

LAKE MICHIGAN

LAKE HURON

MONTREAL

LAKE ONTARIO

BOSTON

LAKE ERIE

NEW YORK

CHICAGO

PITTSBURGH
Ft Duquesne

BALTIMORE

NATIONAL ROAD

WASHINGTON

NSAS CITY

VANDALIA

Ohio R.

Boonesborough

ST. LOUIS

W W W W W W W W W
WILDERNESS ROAD
W W W W W W W

Mississippi R.

WATER Tr.

NASHVILLE

tansas R.

NATCHEZ TRACE

CHARLESTON

DE SOTO

NATCHEZ

NEW ORLEANS

W W W W W W W W W   WILDERNESS ROAD
< < < < < < < < <   WATER TRAIL
/ / / / / / / / /   NATIONAL ROAD
~~~~~~~~~   NATCHEZ TRACE

TRAILS

Sizzling pork and boiling coffee smelled mighty good at the end of a long day on the Road. Supper and chores over, old-timers matched tall tales around the fire, and fiddles set young heels tapping.

THE NATIONAL ROAD

Every day thousands of Americans pile into cars and cross-country buses to bowl west on U.S. 40 exactly as Americans a hundred years ago climbed into Conestoga wagons and stagecoaches to follow the same route — only then they called it the National Road or the Cumberland Road or Uncle Sam's Pike. For the section of U.S. 40 from Cumberland, Maryland, to Vandalia, Illinois, is our most historic Federal government highway, dating back to 1815.

Congress approved the route in 1806, the year Lewis and Clark returned from their explorations, astonishingly and triumphantly alive, to rivet the whole country's attention on westward trails. By 1811 contracts for the new road had been let. Then along came a second war with England, the War of 1812, and actual construction work had to be postponed for three years. The Road, though, was worth waiting for, and when the first section between Cumberland, Maryland, and Wheeling, West Virginia, was opened to traffic in 1818, its crushed-stone construction was the pride of the countryside.

But even then the route of the wonderful new road was part of America's history, for through Maryland and Pennsylvania the road makers had followed an old Indian trail called Nemacolin's Path. Over it the frontier scout Christopher Gist had led Virginia's twenty-year-old Major George Washington carrying official letters requesting the French at Fort Duquesne to leave England's Ohio Country. Young Daniel Boone had toiled over it, too, disgustedly eating dust in the rear of Braddock's army while British engineers hacked at the red man's trail to widen it for caissons and supply wagons.

Nowadays, if a tourist cares to park his car and tramp through Maryland pastures near Grantsville, he will find unused sections of Braddock's famous road still 12 feet wide and, in spots, still paved with the blocks of local stone English soldiers tugged and hauled into place. Even now, according to the old folks, the campfires of the doomed army light the hills on July nights, and ghostly foragers in the scarlet uniforms of British Regulars and the blue of Virginia Rangers raid barnyards.

In those earlier days, travelers nearing Somerfield, Pennsylvania, stopped to see General Braddock's grave or the ruins of Fort Necessity, where Washington fired the first shots of the French and Indian War. Modern tourists visit the restored fort in the National Battlefield Park or pause at the Braddock Monument. The monument was not erected until 1913, but in 1804 workmen repairing the former military road nailed a board lettered "Braddock's Grave" on an elm. Under its branches they had conscientiously reburied the skeleton and the handful of military buttons their spades had dug out of the original grave where fleeing infantrymen had buried their general.

Legend and adventure rode the pike with traffic from the beginning. In fact, sometimes just traveling the National Road must have been adventure enough for anyone. Between 1825 and 1833 contractors had carried it on through Ohio, but by that time, the older part was so badly in need of repair that riding over it tested the mettle of man, beast, and wagon. One Englishman claimed that he had driven across the St. Gothard Alps but that "threading the intricacies of the National Road" was "the more difficult feat of the two!" Even after Congress turned the Road over to the states through which it passed to maintain by tolls, its condition was always unpredictable. But good or bad, Uncle Sam's Pike was a boon to the swelling tide of Americans bound west to Ohio, In-

46

Like their Madonna of the Trail on the National Road, D.A.R. markers indicate the route of many American historic trails.

diana, and Illinois. Kentucky's Indian-fighting Simon Kenton, who founded Springfield, Ohio, in 1799 before the Road existed, would have thought emigrants with any kind of highway under their feet were mighty pampered.

Probably the women in the six families he led would have been frankly envious. Travel was hazardous at best in those early days, but, in linsey and calico, women followed their men. Europeans traveling along the National Road to see America's sights described crude carts loaded 12 feet high with bedding, and women and children roosting on top.

Luckily, America's pioneer women took privations and dangers in their stride, or the country never would have been settled. They reared their families in covered wagons, cooked over campfires, washed out what clothes they could when they found a stream, and cared for sick and injured men and children. When an epidemic struck a wagon train, there was no doctor conveniently in reach of a telephone call. The Bible and the "doctor-book" were a frontier woman's most priceless possessions, but she could use a rifle if she needed to, or risk her life to save a garrison.

The story of Elizabeth Zane of Wheeling was legendary on the Pike. During the Revolution, when beleaguered Fort Henry needed a volunteer to try to bring in fresh supplies of powder, it was Elizabeth who slipped out of the palisades. Every rifleman was needed, she knew, and with food running low, her loss would merely mean one less mouth to feed. The British and their Indian allies surrounded the garrison, but somehow Elizabeth Zane got through and the siege was lifted.

Quite unlike the Wilderness Road and the Oregon Trail, of course, the National Road offered emigrants a string of inns to choose from, and many families took advantage of them, at least to stop for news or buy provisions or get a handful of stogies, those queerly twisted, long, thin smokes that took their name from Conestoga wagons. A whole Spanish cigar cost three cents; even half a cigar cost half a cent, but a man could buy a hundred stogies for twelve cents. George Black, who owned a tiny tobacco store in Washington, Pennsylvania, had invented them from watching wagoners drive along the Road smoking twists of green tobacco yanked off their loads.

Some of the inns catered especially to wagoners, and others to drovers whose flocks of geese and turkeys, or herds of horses, mules, beeves, sheep, and pigs tangled traffic into fantastic snarls. More than 72,000 pigs went over Uncle Sam's Pike in 1835! Most of

48

Heavy loads, blazing sun, rain, mud, and rutted trails kept the wagon trains busy with repairs.

them were half-wild woods hogs, long in leg and snout, used to rooting acorns in timber patches, and ugly-mean animals to cross. But they fed America, for pork was the staple meat in our diet until the vast Longhorn herds began to come over the Chisholm Trail at the end of the Civil War. Whatever a man's occupation might be, however, if he was a seasoned traveler, he kept an eye out for an inn with a fat house dog. Scraps enough to make a dog fat meant plenty of food on the dining room tables!

There was always something doing at an inn, too. Stagecoach companies had ticket offices in the public rooms. Mail carriers brought the latest papers. Peddlers on horseback paused to hawk patent medicines or clocks or tinware. Traveling circuses stopped and set up their cages of lions and bears in the innyard. Itinerant

49

magicians did tricks. Missionaries preached from the Book. And, more rarely, a doctor even opened shop to set a bone or cleanse a festered wound.

But not every frontier doctor devoted all his time to medicine. One of the most famous robbers on the National Road was a physician, Dr. John F. Braddee, and the man who caught him was another physician who liked being a secret agent for the Post Office Department much better than taking care of patients! Braddee had been hostler in a Kentucky inn and choreboy for Dr. Gunn, who had written the frontier's favorite doctor-book, before he came riding into Uniontown, Maryland, driving a herd of horses. Obviously he liked the town. He settled down, opened a medical office, married his first "grateful patient," and proclaimed that he was ready to cure "all diseases in the catalogue." It certainly paid to advertise! Patients came all the way from Massachusetts and New Orleans to be cured by his Cancer Salve or his Cordial Balm of Health. On the side, meanwhile, he tried his hand at counterfeiting.

But it was mail robbery that finally put the handsome doctor in jail. His office window looked over a fence into Lucius Stockton's stage yards where that wealthy "land admiral's" great fleets of coaches were built and repaired and where the mails were transferred. Western merchants and bankers had no way to send money for their Eastern transactions except by mail stage along the National Road, and a stage often carried $50,000, sometimes even $100,000.

Bribery persuaded a stage driver to pass mailbags stuffed with cash through that fence from time to time, and his own assistant to garner them in on the office side. Undoubtedly Dr. Braddee took care to do the hiding of them by himself! But he had failed to reckon with the perseverance of special postal agents. His house was raided; $10,000 was found in the stable and sacks of money in a vault in the yard.

Naturally, with mail stages carrying money in such large qantities, the "gentlemen of the road" found mail bags tempting, but that did not mean they were likely to overlook passengers' pocketbooks. One heavily wooded, gloomy stretch of the Road was a favorite spot for stagecoach holdups. Drivers called it the "Shades of Death," and passengers spent their time trying to dream up new hiding places for their money until they got safely past.

From their point of view, a stagecoach driver was usually enough to cope with without having to worry about highwaymen, too. Racing, of course, was strictly forbidden by stage companies and state law but, law or no law, a driver was not letting a rival overhaul his coach. Peter Burdine of the Good Intent Lines started cracking his whip the minute he caught a glimpse of Redding Bunting driving a National Road Stage Company coach. Probably it did not soothe their passengers' nerves any either when drivers boasted they could turn a coach and four on a silver dollar! James Reeside, owner of the Good Intent Lines, swore his men were the most careful coachmen on the Road, but the Red Admiral (so called from the vests he wore to match his coaches!) was fonder of speed than most of his passengers. If a mail run had been taking twenty-three hours, he liked to get it down to twelve.

The gaudy stages with their painted panels — "General Jackson" had a portrait of the general in buff and gold and green, and "Buckeye" boasted Ohio scenery — have vanished with the chuckholes from Uncle Sam's Pike. State troopers on U.S. 40 would make short work of the highwaymen and footpads of the nineteenth century. But one thing has never changed: there is still a tale for every mile of the road. And if you listen carefully above the rumble of Maryland thunder, you can still hear old Tickle Britches, the giant Negro conjure man, playing tunes on his ghostly violin.

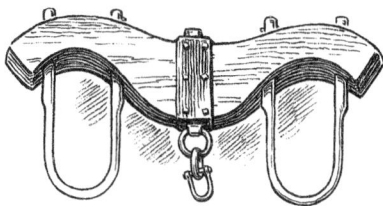

At fords, Indians often added to the troubles of Santa Fe traders struggling to rescue goods and to right a wagon toppled by a steep bank or a swollen river. For years Comanche raids made the Cimarron Crossing one of the most dangerous spots on the Trail.

SANTA FE TRAIL

The modern Santa Fe Trail is made of steel rails running out of Kansas City, where once the bustling frontier town of Westport on the Missouri outfitted Yankee traders, but for long miles the railroad and the remains of the old Trail run side by side. In their comfortable streamliners, with the historical markers on the original Trail flashing by, passengers can watch the Arkansas without a worry over toppling at the river's ford, and listen lazily to the sound of their engine climbing through the Raton Pass, where panting men with bulging muscles once hauled Conestoga wagons foot by foot, a bare 2 miles a day. Yet even today, nearly three-quarters of a century after the first train came rolling in to Santa Fe to end the usefulness of the Trail, travelers can still catch glimpses of the ruts furrowed by the heavy wagons that used to creak and sway along it in the dangerous commerce of the prairies.

In the old days it was six long weeks — forty days and 800 miles — out of Franklin or Independence or Westport, Missouri, before the Santa Fe Trail came to an end at the sun-baked adobe walls of the little Spanish town for which it was named. The Santa Fe was the first of our great transcontinental trails, but it was old before the white man ever came to America. It was a trail of the buffalo and of the Indians who hunted them for food and clothing and lodge skins. Later it was a trail for Spaniard, Mexican, and Frenchman; later still for Yankee trapper, trader, and soldier. After the discovery of gold and silver, folks bound for California and Colorado sometimes followed it, too, and our Army

53

of the West knew it well, but primarily the Santa Fe Trail was a trade route, linking the color and gaiety of the old Spanish towns and the brash swagger of the lusty, young American West. Over it the caravans jolted, across Kansas, along the Arkansas River, into the southeast corner of Colorado, then over the Raton Pass into the Rockies, or, if the wagon master preferred, across the desert cutoff, the terrible Jornado, 60 waterless, mirage-filled miles from the Cimarron Crossing on the Arkansas to the Cimarron River, and through the northwest corner of Oklahoma. The Jornado, Hornather to the traders, was shorter and more level, but it was also more perilous. Men and animals grew haggard from blistering heat and lack of water. A caravan plodded at a slow 15 to 20 miles a day, and in the desert the pace was often slower — and many a veteran wagon master lost his way. No more experienced, resourceful man ever walked in moccasins than Jedediah Smith, one of the greatest of the fur-trapping Mountain Men, yet he lost his train in the Jornado. Finally, scouting ahead alone, he found the water that saved his men, and lost his own life to the Indians. For in addition to all its other dangers, the desert route lay in Comanche territory. Even thirty years later, in 1861, Indian hostility was so great that the caravans actually had to abandon the Cimarron Crossing.

But whichever way the caravans chose, the desert route from the Cimarron Crossing or the mountain route from Bent's Fort, the Trail united again at the Mora River, and the wagons rolled on — to the Gallinas River and Las Vegas, to Tecolote and Bernal, to the Pecos River and San Miguel, and into Santa Fe.

A caravan for Santa Fe must have looked like a circus parade when it left Missouri — man after man, traders, teamsters, hunters, scouts, sometimes as many as 300, and wagon after loaded wagon, each one weighing 3,000 to 7,000 pounds. Gaudy with red and blue paint, their new canvas dazzling in the sunshine, they lumbered out of Independence or Westport behind a dozen mules or six yoke of oxen, mule skinners or bullwhackers beside their teams or herding the scores of spare animals, replacements for the beasts that would wear out along the way. The wagons were of the strongest possible build, but the Trail and the blazing Southwest sun would send them crawling back in the fall, bleached, warped, and shrunken, the spokes of their wheels and the iron-shod rims tied with rawhide to keep them from falling apart. Of course, there were tricks in trade then, too. The collector of customs in Santa Fe levied a tax on every wagon (in 1837 it rose to $500 on each), so the Yankees stopped a number of miles away and proceeded to do a little carpentry. When they finished, the parts of all the smaller wagons were securely cached, and the big ones creaked on into Santa Fe, suddenly bloated to the most astonishing proportions by wooden additions to hold the extra loads! Fortunately, the road had turned almost respectable by that time, or the top-heavy wagons would have ended wrongside up on the Trail.

As long as Spain ruled the Southwest, the viceroy in Mexico City guarded the lucrative Santa Fe trade jealously, and the occasional French and American trappers or traders who made their way to the muddy little New Mexico town were decidedly unwelcome. In fact, after Lieutenant Zebulon Pike and his expedition trespassed on Spanish territory without permission, *Americanos* were not merely unwelcome, they were jailed. One party of would-be traders actually spent nearly nine years in Mexican jails! But in 1821 Mexican revolutionaries overthrew the rule of Spain, and the situation suddenly changed. Out on the plains a Missourian named William Becknell, his pack horses loaded with goods for the Indian trade, saw a party of Mexican soldiers and got ready for trouble. Instead of a fight, however, he got a cordial invitation to come do his trading in Santa Fe. And five months later he was dumping his profits, big rawhide bags full of Mexican silver dollars, on the sidewalk back in Independence, Missouri. The great days of the Trail had begun.

Becknell himself promptly inserted an alluring ad in the *Missouri Intelligencer* for "men to go westward for the purpose of trad-

Forted up behind the dead mules, Kit
and five Carson men held off 200
mounted Comanches all day.

ing for horses and mules and catching wild animals of every
description," and set out again in 1822. This trip, however, he
was not leading pack horses. Instead, for the first time, an American wagon train rolled up the dust clouds on the Santa Fe Trail.
Only three wagons and thirty-one men, but they have kept Becknell's name alive as "the father of the Santa Fe Trail." Year by
year the trade grew, and come spring, wagon after wagon, loaded
with cottons, woolens, silks, velvets, cutlery, and hardware, jolted
down the Trail, to return in the fall with beaver pelts, buffalo hides,
and Mexican silver. By 1855 the yearly merchandise freighted
over the Trail was valued at $5,000,000, and according to the
records five years later, it took 3,033 wagons, 9,084 men, 6,147
mules, and 27,920 oxen to handle the Santa Fe trade.

The jumping-off place for the caravans, first Franklin, then
Independence, and finally Westport, Missouri, each boomed into
the busiest town west of St. Louis — blacksmith shops clanging
with hammers; pack horses, mules, and oxen milling in the market
corrals; supply stores fit to burst at the seams as men bargained for

56

50 pounds of flour, 50 pounds of bacon, 10 pounds of coffee, 20 pounds of sugar, and a bag of salt to carry with them down the Trail. Then, almost before a town could get used to its growing pains, the steamboats were disgorging California- and Oregon-bound settlers who had to be outfitted, too. To the Santa Fe trader, though, the emigrants were not worth much. He regarded them all with the contempt of the professional for the amateur: "jest askin' to git their hayr lifted," in his opinion, "swarmin' out over the perairies not knowing the hind end of a mewel from the front, or a buffler from a cussed Injun."

They were an undisciplined lot, these traders, self-confident, opinionated, aggressive, ready to dare danger to knock the chips off their shoulders. And danger came often on the Santa Fe Trail, in wilting heat and agonizing thirst in the Jornado; in the sharp thrust of a Comanche lance at a water hole; in a stampede of terri-fied oxen, stranding a train 400 miles from nowhere; in shouted orders "Corral! Corral! Fort up!" as red-skinned raiders thun-dered down on the wagons from behind the sandhills.

A caravan in any kind of trouble could generally count on Indian trouble, too, and as the volume of traffic on the Trail in-creased, Indian hostility grew. Where wagon trains went, they figured, soldiers and forts and settlers followed eventually, and game disappeared. In 1847, they took advantage of our war with Mexico to attack every train on the Trail. Even an army escort was no guarantee of safety, and Lieutenant Love, with his eighty dragoons, carrying pay for American troops and convoying thirty traders, was lucky to escape with only eleven casualties. Another train lost 160 oxen worth $4,000 in half an hour, not to mention loaded wagons worth another $7,000 abandoned for lack of teams. Kit Carson himself was waylaid that season! All in all, the loss on the Trail for that year alone amounted to 47 killed, 330 wagons destroyed or abandoned, and 6,500 head of stock run off or killed. The end of the Mexican War and the treaty which gave us posses-sion of the old Spanish southwest doomed the Indian's way of life,

57

but he did not give it up without a struggle. Forty years later the Army of the West was still fighting Indians, but in the later days of the Santa Fe Trail small military supply forts at least made the way somewhat easier for the caravans.

Still, for men whose scalps had been prickling for two or three hundred miles and whose wagons had been traveling four abreast for easier "forting up," one of the most cheerful sights on the whole Trail must have been Bent's Old Fort, for years the only building between Missouri and the Mexican settlements. Erected on the Arkansas about 5 miles beyond Horse Creek on the mountain route to Santa Fe, its gray adobe walls, 15 feet high, had loopholes along the top and bastions, portholed for cannon, towering over them. Its wicketed gates, sheathed in iron and studded with enormous nails, were built in under a square blockhouse. The walls, of course, enclosed a big patio with a well sweep and a robe press, where folded hides were crushed flat and tied for shipment, and the long, whitewashed adobe buildings used for storerooms, offices, and living quarters. The fort boasted twenty-two bedrooms, but to the men from the Trail the most impressive thing was the smell of the only biscuits between Westport and California, floating out of the kitchen!

In the fur trade, the Astors alone rivaled the firm of Bent and St. Vrain, and back in St. Louis the partners donned high beaver hats and frock coats. Out here on the plains, though, they wore fringed hunting shirts and moccasins like Indian chiefs. Their posts were scattered from Fort St. Vrain near Long's Peak in Colorado to Adobe Walls down on the Canadian River in the Texas Panhandle, but biggest of them all was the Old Fort on the Arkansas, where William Bent lived and managed the trade with the Plains Indians. At least a hundred clerks, traders, teamsters, packers, hunters, and servants were on the payroll at a time — violent men most of them, but no one was ever killed within the walls of the Old Fort. William Bent, "with eyes like augurs and a jaw like a steel trap," knew how to handle trouble!

58

What's more, the Bents had no Indian trouble either, in spite of the fact that William was married to a daughter of Gray Thunder, Keeper of the Cheyenne Medicine Arrows, which was reason enough for difficulties with the Comanches, Apaches, and Kiowas. All the Plains Indians, however, seem to have trusted and respected the Bents. Just the same, with a thousand horse-loving Indians within striking distance, William took precautions. The wall around the corral attached to the Old Fort was 3 feet thick by 8 feet high and topped by growing cactus!

In the pioneer Southwest the Old Fort was combination bank, home, and general store for hundreds, and sooner or later it saw every man who left his mark on the Santa Fe Trail. It burst a cannon saluting the Army of the West when General Stephen Kearny and his Missourians arrived on their way to conquer New Mexico and California. It heard the trumpets and drums of the famous Mormon Battalion under Jefferson Hunt and Philip St. George Cooke. Old Bill Gary (William Guerrier) in his white blanket coat and fur cap was one of its traders. Lucien Maxwell, whose silver tableware made men's eyes pop and whose herds of cattle, sheep, and horses were constantly in sight for 45 miles along the Trail, was once its foreman. The Sublette brothers, Tom Fitzpatrick, and other Mountain Men made it a rendezvous, and Kit Carson was one of its hunters.

Kit was a stocky, sandy-haired bound boy in trouble with his master in Independence when Tom Fitzpatrick helped him run away, and it was for the Bent caravan on the Santa Fe Trail that he headed astride his family's old mule. Kit was never a big man, and though he became Colonel and even General Carson among the whites, to the Indians he was always Little Chief, the name the Cheyennes gave him after he had trailed and attacked a war party of fifty Crows with a dozen of his men to recapture the Bent horses they had stolen. A fight with fifty Crows was nothing in Kit Carson's life, however. Down in the Cimarron Country he and five of his men held off 200 mounted Comanches all day, and finally

The travois (two poles generally joined by a framework of buffalo hide and hitched to a horse) was the Plains Indians' moving van.

made them give up in disgust. Kit had just organized his own band of trappers then, the original six — Kit and Joe Meek, Bill Mitchell and the three Delaware Indians, Jonas, Tom Hill, and Manhead — who were the nucleus of the famous band known later as the Carson Men. Not one of them was over twenty-five, and Jonas was still in his teens, but Kit had known what he was doing when he chose his men. They killed their mules and forted up behind them, firing in relays at the charging Comanches and digging in with knives and hatchets whenever there was a lull. Fortunately for them, the smell of the dead mules worked the way Kit had hoped. It drove the Comanche ponies crazy and they bucked so wildly the warriors could hardly launch their arrows.

The old single-shot rifle was a useful weapon, of course, but it had drawbacks. Though an Indian on horseback could loose an arrow every two seconds, it was next to impossible for a white man to fire his rifle, reload, and handle his mount at the same time. Mountain Men like Kit's band, trained to fort up and fire in relays,

60

stood a chance of holding mounted Indians off, but they had to be superb shots and cool as ice to do it. For the Plains Indians had not been slow to learn that they could ride or lance the white man down the minute he fired his rifle. The first repeater, the Colt revolving-breech pistol, which spewed lead right and left and could be loaded and fired in the saddle, must have jolted the Indians considerably when they met it about 1841. The Texas Rangers claim the distinction of taming the Comanches with the Colt, but Carson Men, riding half the night to rescue a wagon train forted against Kiowas, were the first to use it on the Santa Fe Trail.

The old Trail was full of flavor, and that flavor got into the personalities of the men who cussed the dust and the Indians and the high taxes of the Mexican governors. It got into hundreds as it got into Kit Carson and into Richens Wootten, Uncle Dick to stagecoach passengers, who finally settled down to build and keep the toll road over the Raton Pass, and into Alexander Majors, who made his men "agree not to use profane language" and earned a fortune freighting out of Independence. It was a Majors train, incidentally, that figured in the famous story of the caravan overtaken and passed by the mail stage, only to get into Santa Fe first. The stage fell foul of Indians, of course, and the wagons, plodding along days later, found its charred fragments. The people who used the Santa Fe Trail were few compared to the thousands who followed the northern trails to California and Oregon; the value of its trade, small compared to the wealth of goods freighted to Salt Lake City; but perhaps more than any other trail, it still stirs the imagination to adventure as it did when the giants of our Western history followed its ruts.

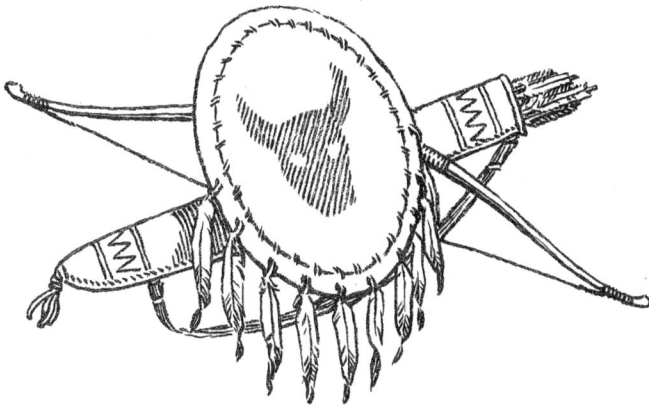

The men of the Lewis and Clark expedition floundered over quicksand and waded through icy water up to their waists, cordelling their boat against stubborn currents. Ashore, their hunters were just as busy trying to find enough food for the hearty appetites of the Corps of Discovery.

OREGON TRAIL

Overland Trail to Oregon, California, and Great Salt Lake

People sometimes say that the Overland Trail to Oregon, California, and the Great Salt Lake was just a double set of wagon tracks across the continent, but in the boom days of the California gold rush, when as many as two or three dozen trains of a hundred wagons each "jumped off" simultaneously, literally dozens of wheel ruts stretched as far as a man could see toward the West. Trains constantly drove past each other; wagons passed and repassed, shifting positions in their own train, all of them converging again for water holes and river fords and mountain passes. In time, too, trail-blazing pioneers developed alternate routes and cutoffs. But the great parent Trail struck off into the wilderness from one of the busy outfitting towns on the Missouri, Independence or Westport, to follow the Santa Fe Trail for nearly 40 miles and then turn northwest to the Platte, where the wagons creaked along the river to the junction of the North Platte and the South Platte. Fording the South Plate, the trains could again follow a river, the North Platte, to Fort Laramie, and then strike out for what is now Casper, Wyoming, cross the mountains by the famous broad, level South Pass to the basin of the Colorado River, and turn southwest to Fort Bridger. There the Overland Trail divided, the section known as the Mormon Trail continuing southeast to the Great Salt Lake and the Oregon Trail going northwest to Fort Hall on the Snake River, where the parent Trail again split two ways, the California Trail branching off to the southwest and the Oregon Trail keeping

63

on to Fort Boise and the long, hard climb over the Blue Mountains. Once beyond the mountains, though, the worst was over. Trail-frayed tempers grew sweet again, and the wagons trundled on to Fort Walla Walla and down the south bank of the Columbia River into the beautiful Willamette Valley, the center of the early settlements in the Oregon Country. The end of the trail shifted, of course, as settlement spread, and though in popular stories Astoria is probably still oftenest called the "end," the Trail eventually reached Tumwater, Washington, and one branch went up to Olympia and the Puget Sound country.

Over this great transcontinental trail went thousands upon thousands of people much too busy at the job of living to stop to consider that they were creating a nation out of a wilderness: explorers, trappers, fur traders, U.S. cavalrymen going to fight Indians, Protestant and Catholic missionaries, Mormons, emigrant farmers bound for free land in Oregon, gold-seeking Forty-niners, stagecoach drivers and Pony Express riders. But to one of those busy pioneers, Ezra Meeker (born in Ohio, 1830; died in Seattle, Washington, 1928) the modern motorist actually owes the fact that he can still find markers for the Overland Trail on U.S. 30 and 40.

In the early spring of 1852 twenty-two-year-old Meeker and his young wife had picked up their baby, packed their belongings, and joined an emigrant train at Council Bluffs, the first stop on the route beyond the Missouri. By October the train had reached the Oregon Country, and the Meekers had reached "home." Time did not hang heavy on pioneer hands, but as the years went by, Ezra managed to salvage enough to learn everything he could about the history of the Pacific Northwest. He had had just two or three months of school in his whole life; yet sooner than most of his contemporaries, he recognized the importance to the United States of the great migrations across the plains. The more he thought about it, the more important it seemed to mark the route of the great Trail before it was entirely lost. So, at the age of seventy-six, he set out in an ox-drawn covered wagon from his home in Puyallup, Wash-

64

Sane explorers tried to avoid the great
humped-back, dish-faced grizzly who
could carry off a bull and, on its hind legs,
reach 12 feet into the air.

ington, following the parts of the Trail still open, painting inscrip-
tions on landmarks, and urging the towns along the way to set up
monuments. But Ezra Meeker did not stop at the old outfitting
towns on the Missouri. Like Barnum, he was a born showman,
and, still in his covered wagon, he toured the East, stirring up en-
thusiasm for marking the Trail wherever he went. In 1910 he
repeated his performance, and five years later the old gentleman
behind the goggles, jolting over the Trail in a newfangled, 1915-
model touring car, turned out to be Ezra Meeker again. By the
time he was ninety-three he was flying over the Trail in an airplane,
and two years later he had succeeded in founding the Oregon Trail
Memorial Association, with headquarters in New York City. In
fact, until a few months before his death at the age of ninety-eight,

Ezra Meeker was still following the old route, and to him belongs the major credit for the nationwide celebration in 1930 of the first use of wagons on the Trail to Oregon.

Certainly that was something to celebrate. For never in history, except in the great years of the Overland Trail, has so vast a territory as the American West been settled in so short a time by so many. Captain Bonneville of fur-trade fame took the first wagons over South Pass in 1832, and two smallish emigrant trains went up the Trail in 1841 and 1842, the first led to California by John Bidwell and the second to Oregon by Elijah White. But a year later Jesse Applegate shepherded 900 people and 1,000 head of livestock to Oregon in the "Great Migration," and by 1845 the emigrants on the Trail totaled 3,000 men, women, and children. Even before the California gold rush, America was going West in a hurry. And when the Forty-niners hit the Trail, 35,000 people crossed the continent in a single year! It had taken two hundred years to push our frontiers westward from the Atlantic seaboard up the river valleys and across the Alleghenies to the Mississippi. It took only fifty to people the land from the Mississippi all the way to the Pacific.

But back in the early years of the nineteenth century Americans knew little of the lands beyond the mighty river. Nobody even knew how much of those lands our new Louisiana Purchase included, and, in the East, many a citizen was sure we had been royally rooked paying Napoleon that $15,000,000. President Thomas Jefferson, however, had no doubts about its value. Long before the Purchase had been dreamed of, his thoughts had been turning west. Even when he took office, he was already considering the possibility of a government exploring expedition beyond the Mississippi, not then, of course — just sometime — but he was careful to choose as his private secretary a young neighbor of his from Virginia, Capt. Meriwether Lewis of the U.S. Infantry. President Jefferson was taking no chances! When the time did come for his expedition, he intended to have the best man in the

United States for the job of leader right where he could lay his hands on him.

Then in 1803, even before the Louisiana Purchase was settled, Congress did authorize the expedition; President Jefferson promptly picked Meriwether Lewis as its captain, and Captain Lewis chose his former comrade-in-arms, William Clark, to be co-captain. During the Revolution, William's brother, George Rogers Clark, had done the impossible and captured Kaskaskia and Vincennes — and William was as redheaded as George. Perhaps Captain Lewis had heard the old Clark family saying, that every redheaded Clark was born to distinguish himself! At any rate, he picked the right man, and President Jefferson had reason to be satisfied with both his commanders. Clark was a sufficiently skillful draughtsman to prepare maps and scientific drawings; Lewis had not only boned up on navigation but was amateur scientist enough to make accurate observations and collect specimens to bring back; both of them were born leaders and experienced frontiersmen and Indian fighters, and, just as important to the success of the expedition, they were congenial friends who knew how to work together. In the three years of their joint command, in a journey across a continent and back under conditions that would have strained most friendships, through danger, discouragement, hunger, thirst, sickness, and suffering, Lewis and Clark differed only in their opinion of the charms of dog stew in Indian villages! Lewis was pro when he was hungry enough; Clark was anti even then.

In May of 1804, a keelboat and two pirogues pushed out from shore and headed up the Missouri "to search out a land route to the Pacific and gather information about the Indians and the country of the Far West." The Lewis and Clark expedition was on its way. Moreover, it no longer needed the passports President Jefferson had obtained from the French minister, for the Louisiana Purchase was signed, sealed, and delivered. They were off up an *American* river to explore *American* territory — off with twenty-one bales of presents for the Indians and Private Cruzat's violin.

67

Tipis of the Plains Indians.

Admittedly the boats were also packed with supplies of food, clothing, tools, medicines, and ammunition, but Private Cruzat's violin, like the Indian presents, was one of the biggest assets of the expedition. It fascinated the Indians and it took care of everybody's favorite amusement. For feminine partners or no feminine partners, the Lewis and Clark men square-danced clear to the Pacific! Apparently a day's journey had to be mighty ornery before they were too tired to want dance tunes.

It was at the first winter quarters in the Mandan villages, however, 1,500 miles from the starting point at St. Louis, that its most remarkable member joined the "Corps of Discovery." Sacajawea, Bird Woman, was a young Shoshone girl who had been captured by the Hidatsa several years before and who was now squaw to a French-Canadian trapper, Toussaint Charbonneau. Charbonneau's shortcomings stuck out like the quills on a porcupine, but he had been in Indian country ten years, and both captains realized that he and his squaw would make a valuable interpreting team.

68

Among the Indians along the river, Charbonneau would have his uses, and in the Rocky Mountain area, Sacajawea's Shoshone would help. Back on the Mississippi, while the expedition was outfitting and training, Lewis and Clark had talked to everyone who might have information about the land to the west — merchants in St. Louis, traders and trappers who drifted into town, and probably Daniel Boone, too, living nearby at St. Charles as trail-wise and lively as ever. They knew enough to value Charbonneau's little squaw. Consequently, when the Corps of Discovery left the Mandans in the spring to begin their real job of exploration, Sacajawea, with her tiny papoose strapped to its board on her back, meekly followed her husband and the strange white men toward the West.

The Corps of Discovery boasted as dauntless and remarkable a group of men as ever took to the wilderness trails George Drouilliard, skilled woodsman and shrewd interpreter; Reuben and Joseph Fields, crack Kentucky shots who knew how to live off the country; competent Sergeant Gass, whose carefully kept journal is still valuable reading; John Shields, who set up a blacksmith shop and hammered out tomahawks to win friends for the expedition in the Rockies; Clark's Negro slave, York, who finally returned to the West and became an important man among the Crows; John Potts and John Colter, who chose to remain in the Rockies when the rest went home. Apparently dangers only fascinated Potts and Colter. Both Lewis and Clark picked them for especially hazardous jobs, and in their later trapping days, it was Colter, alone and on foot, with a 30-pound pack on his back, his gun, and some ammunition, who discovered and explored what we now call Yellowstone Park — "Colter's Hell" in those days.

But none of them was braver, harder-working, or more uncomplaining, useful, and faithful than the small Shoshone squaw. To the last enlisted man, the Corps of Discovery admired and respected the patient courage of Sacajawea, who somehow cajoled horses and guides through the mountains out of the reluctant Shoshones and managed to warn Captain Lewis every time her long-lost brother, Chief Ca-me-âh-wait, changed his mind about helping them — which was at least once every other day! Captain Clark grew genuinely fond of Charbonneau's squaw and of her small papoose Baptiste, whom he cheerfully nicknamed "Pomp." Later, when Clark was governor of the Missouri Territory, he saw to Baptiste's education in St. Louis, and though the young man won the friend-ship of Prince Paul of Wuertemberg and visited with him in Europe, he returned again to the West to serve as guide for many travelers, including Captain Clark's son, Jefferson.

But even Sacajawea's usefulness never reconciled the Corps of Discovery to her tribe's system of greeting callers. "They take us round the neck and Sweze us in Stead of shakeing hands," Sargeant Gass complained in his journal, and fastidious Captain Lewis, suf-fering acutely, lamented that "we wer all carresed and besmeared with their grease and paint till I was heartily sick of the national hug." Still, that was nothing to what poor York had to endure. He was a constant source of astonishment and admiration to the Indians, but everywhere the expedition went, some chief promptly got busy licking his finger and scrubbing away at York's arm to make sure his color was really indelible!

Meanwhile, back in the States, as two years passed, hope for the Lewis and Clark expedition dwindled. No official word had come in since they left the Mandan villages — only a message from some Osage chiefs that the expedition had actually crossed the Rockies. Somewhere in the silence beyond the mountains the Corps of Discovery had vanished; no one would ever know where. One dismal rumor claimed they had all been tomahawked, and another reported them Spanish captives, slaving away in the Mex-ican mines! Then, on September 23, 1806, to the astonished de-light of the entire United States, the Corps of Discovery landed happily in the center of St. Louis. In spite of lice, fleas, rattle-snakes, grizzly bears and dog stew, angry Sioux and still angrier Blackfeet, they had crossed the continent a second time. "In

Over snowy passes.

obedience to your orders we have penetrated the continent of North America to the Pacific Ocean," Lewis wrote in a hasty scrawl to Jefferson. Now they had come home.

The Lewis and Clark expedition stirred the nation. They were not the first explorers to cross to the Pacific; on July 22, 1793, the Canadian Alexander Mackenzie had painted his name on a rock on the Coast after a trip that was a monument to his courage, his endurance, and his mastery of men. But the effect of their exploration on the opening of our West was incalculable. Other government expeditions followed them, notably Long's, Nicollet's and Frémont's, and slowly the knowledge of the country west of the Mississippi grew. Lewis and Clark had traveled an Eastern river and then tried to follow a Western one, but the navigable rivers always led into the most impassable mountains peaks. Later ex-

71

plorers finally gave up the rivers and tried to find an open way across the country farther south. The result of their combined efforts, of course, was the Overland Trail, and woe to the wagon trains whose leaders lost or left the route. Twenty miles to the east or west, and they ended in a tangle of mountain peaks and chasms from which they would be lucky to emerge alive.

Military men like Dodge, Leavenworth, and Atkinson officially picked up geographical information as they roamed the plains trying to deal with the Indians; Henry Schoolcraft, Indian agent at Mackinac, discovered Lake Itasca, source of the Mississippi; John Jacob Astor's fur traders crossed the country to establish his post at Astoria, but no government expedition followed Lewis and Clark across the mountains until after 1840, perhaps because we had no exclusive interest in the Oregon Country. For, by the old treaties, England and the United States shared joint settlement rights until President Polk's efforts, after 1845, finally straightened out the boundary problem. In 1842, however, John C. Frémont's official expedition finally explored the Rockies, and in 1843, his second went all the way to Oregon, nosed about the Nevada country, and crossed the Sierras to California. It is still easy to start an argument about Frémont's ability as an explorer. Even in his own day some people claimed he was better at boasting than pathfinding, but the young lieutenant's enthusiastic reports of what he had seen in the land beyond the mountains certainly helped spread the "Oregon fever" that soon set emigrant train after emigrant train to swaying westward.

At any rate, nobody has ever wasted time debating the skill of Frémont's guides. For any explorer who managed to get hold of Lucien Maxwell and Kit Carson for one trip and Tom Fitzpatrick and then Kit again for the second was playing in luck from the start. Down the Trail to Santa Fe, overland across the plains, along the Gila by the old Spanish routes to California — it made no difference to Mountain Men like these who had hunted and trapped for Bent and St. Vrain from the Cimarron clear across the country. Like the army, the enormous fur trade had opened new regions farther and farther afield. But it was not just the thought of a fortune in pelts that set a Mountain Man's feet itching for new trails. It was the lure of the wilderness and the memory of smoke rising from lonely campfires. A man could always cache his skins and go a bit farther. A Crow chief claimed there was a pass through the mountains yonder. It wouldn't hurt any to go see. And that was pretty much what happened in 1824 when Jedediah Smith and Tom Fitzpatrick rediscovered famous South Pass in southern Wyoming. Robert Stuart, returning from John Jacob Astor's Astoria, close to the old site of Lewis and Clark's little Fort Clatsop on the Pacific, had led his men through South Pass in 1812, and apparently no one happened to stumble on it again for twelve years. Finally, Mountain Men made the route known to the wagon trains, and Tom Fitzpatrick, James Bridger, and Joe Meek all served as guides through the Pass.

Joe Meek had not changed much either since the days when he helped Kit Carson stand off those 200 Comanches in the Cimarron Country. He was still reckless enough to make it a miracle he had not lost nine lives, and nobody yet had beaten him at tall stories. To the space-loving, footloose Mountain Men the end of the trapping era seemed like the end of the world, but Joe Meek tried to settle down on a farm by the Willamette River where the town of Hillsboro, Oregon, eventually grew up. Not even his best friends could have called him much of a farmer, but it was Joe Meek that Oregon sent racing to Washington, D.C., after the Whitman Massacre.

Narcissa Whitman, traveling with her doctor husband, was one of the first two white women to follow the Trail to the Oregon Country, where the Whitmans settled down in 1836 to raise their family and minister to the Indians from the mission they founded at Waiilatpu. A tourist in Walla Walla, Washington, today can visit the national monument marking the spot where the Whitman mission flourished for eleven years, but toward the end of 1847, when Cayuse Indians wiped out the entire Whitman family and everyone else at the mission station, Oregon settlers were not worrying about being interesting to twentieth-century visitors. They were worrying about their scalps. The Cayuses had never been friendly, and the Whitman Massacre might be the start of Indian war.

It was January when Joe Meek left for Washington to ask Federal aid; snow was piled deep in the mountain passes and the plains were bitter — but he got through. What's more, he thoroughly enjoyed himself, especially whenever he reached a settlement where he could tell the startled citizens that he was "envoy extraordinary and minister plenipotentiary from the Republic of Oregon to the Court of the United States!" According to his own tale, he was "ragged, dirty, and lousy" when he reached Washington in May, but it certainly did not seem to bother anybody. Joe was a spectacular success, warmly welcomed and promptly called "Colonel" by everyone he met. Moreover, when Congress passed the Oregon bill, making a territory of our Pacific Northwest, it was "Colonel Meek" whom President Polk appointed its first U.S. marshal.

It is not hard to see how valuable a Mountain Man like Joe Meek could be to an emigrant train. Caravans freighting goods to Santa Fe or over the plains to Salt Lake were loaded and manned by experienced men. But the Oregon-bound farmers were usually greenhorns. In the wake of their prairie schooners the plains were strewn with trunks and furniture, dumped to lighten their loads, for their wagons often were piled so full they either jolted to pieces on the Trail or could not be hauled over the mountains. Wolves chewed their harness to shreds; Indians stampeded their livestock; their oxen fell exhausted by the wayside. They had to learn the hard way, but most of them learned, and by the time a train reached South Pass, many a pioneer stoically sawed his wagon through the middle into two carts and scrapped everything he had started with except his family and the food he had left.

The Forty-niners had even more to learn; thousands of them

74

had never seen anything more rural than a city pavement! Gold was discovered in California in the summer of 1848. By late September Eastern newspapers were full of stories of nuggets. lying around like acorns under California oaks, and before March of '49, 20,000 people were waiting to "jump off" from Independence, Council Bluffs, Fort Leavenworth, and St. Joseph. Frontier stores did a landslide business in guidebooks, saddles, ox yokes, rope, bull whips, flour, bacon, coffee, tobacco, and guns — though a good half of the gun-toters were a lot more likely to shoot themselves than an Indian. When April came, off they went, gee-hawing up the trail in time to feed their animals on the first May grass of the plains. Some men hung their possessions like a blanket roll across their shoulders and shuffled along on foot. One Scotsman shoved

Whooping down to scare the green-horns on the trail was a favorite amuse-ment of the friendly young bucks.

his belongings ahead of him in a wheelbarrow! But people with money bought two or three covered wagons, and most people with less money worked their way with a train.

And in 1849 the trains on the Trail made nearly a continuous procession, the lead oxen of one snorting into the chicken coop lashed behind the last wagon of the train ahead. Fords at the rivers were bedlam. Wagons broke out of line to race for the best springs and camping grounds. Trains, driving around each other, buried animals and wagons in dust. Train captains, elected at the "jumping-off" spots before the start, tore their hair and cussed, for unruly Forty-niners and congestion on the Trail turned their attempts at disciplined travel into a joke. But at least as long as they were in dangerous Indian country, they remembered to fort up in a hollow square whenever they stopped. At night, animals were turned loose to graze until dark; then herders drove them into the safe square of the wagons. Inside the barricade children played while supper sizzled over the campfires, and later people visited from wagon to wagon, exchanging news and gossip. Sometimes a wedding set fiddles scraping and feet to dancing under the stars. But, come morning, they were up with the sun; the Trail and another day with its regulation 15 miles of hard travel lay ahead. Luckily for all of them, too, the grass was good in '49, since by June 23 the actual count of wagons that had passed Fort Kearney on the Platte already totaled 5,516, and one of the Mormon leaders estimated that 60,000 head of stock crossed the plains in addition to the animals in his own train.

The Mormons, of course, already driven from settlement to settlement, were old hands at wagon travel when Brigham Young led his vanguard over the Trail to their final location in the valley of the Great Salt Lake. The Mormon leader was practical as well as pious, and he established "stations" to rest livestock and repair wagons along their route for the benefit of the trains of his Latter-day Saints still to follow. Marching orders came at morning prayers. Men must walk beside their own wagons and not stray

76

A hunter with a deer.

off to get into arguments and quarrels. Brigham Young had small patience, also, with wasting time while the bugler and half a dozen men searched for some hunter who had got himself lost. The Mormons endured the same hardships others endured on the Trail; sometimes their tongues swelled with thirst, and their skins cracked open from the alkali dust; sometimes their tempers flared; but their trains moved with more disciplined order.

On July 22, 1847, Young's vanguard reached their valley, held a prayer meeting, and unloaded their plows. Two years later when the Forty-niners came over the Trail, Salt Lake City was already flourishing. Water from streams in the Wasatch Mountains ran in irrigation ditches across the desert to the farms. Shade and fruit trees were planted. Community buildings were going up. Ben Holladay, of later stagecoach fame, had hauled in $75,000 worth of goods, and the Mormon Trail through the Wasatch ranges had been a U.S. mail route for a year.

But even in the old West, any other mail route must have seemed tame after riding for the Pony Express, and when a Pony Rider tore by, folks plodding along in emigrant trains must have wanted to say what Mark Twain said about the jack rabbit: "Long after he was out of sight, we could still hear him whiz!" The Pony Express carried mail for only eighteen months, from April 3, 1860, until October, 1861, when telegraph wires from the Atlantic and the Pacific met and ended its usefulness, but never has any other mail service so stirred the imagination of Americans.

It was not a new idea in 1860. Senator William Gwin of California had tried to interest Congress in the idea five years earlier, but nothing had come of it. In fact, in 1858 John Butterfield had been given a contract for a regular mail and stage line over the southern route from St. Louis and Memphis to El Paso and Los Angeles. With civil war threatening, however, Westerners could see that the Butterfield Line might be cut off and communication with California from the north seriously disrupted.

One of the men to whom Senator Gwin mentioned the problem happened to be William Russell, in Washington temporarily on business for his firm, the famous pioneer freighting partnership, Russell, Majors, and Waddell. And William Russell went back to his firm's headquarters at Leavenworth ready to sell his partners the idea. They were not enthusiastic. Alexander Majors seemed to think that even in the days when he was a teamster with a few wagons on the Santa Fe Trail, another teamster named Russell was always ready to promote anything! The news that their rival, Butterfield, was likely to start a pony express on the southern route did not excite Majors and Waddell either. But when Russell hinted that he had practically pledged the firm's word to establish the line,

78

they got busy in a hurry. Russell, Majors, and Waddell had a well-established and well-deserved reputation for honoring its pledges.

From St. Joseph on the Missouri to Sacramento, California — 1,980 miles to be covered in eight to ten days by relays of fast horses and riders! The partners altered their freight route to shave distances; they added new relay stations from Salt Lake to California; they equipped the entire 190 stations on the length of the route with food and horsefeed; they bought 420 horses, most of them blooded stock, tested for speed and stamina; and when the job was done, they had 80 crack riders and 400 relay-station men on their payroll.

Speed was all-important — for the mail and for the safety of the riders. They carried no rifles, only a knife and a revolver. They were not supposed to get off and fight Indians; they were supposed to carry the mail! Flying targets were hard to hit, and Indian ponies were no match for theirs in fleetness or endurance. No rider need apply who weighed more than 135. Rider, saddle, and mail must tote up to no more than 170 pounds; these horses were in a hurry. And 250 miles a day had to be covered! If a station had been attacked by Indians and burned, stock run off, keepers and fresh rider killed, then man and horse rode on to the next station. Pony Bob Haslam once had to ride 380 miles himself, the longest run ever covered by a single rider in the organization, when the Indians were on the warpath. But in all the trips across the continent made by the riders of the Pony Express, in the 650,000 miles they covered in a year and a half, only one mail was ever lost! And for us today, the Pony Express, like the great Trail over which its riders raced, has come to be the symbol of pioneer America.

With a storm brewing, both punchers and ponies had their work cut out to bed down a herd. Trail bosses always chose the most intelligent and best-trained cow ponies on a spread when they trailed Longhorns north to Kansas.

CHISHOLM TRAIL

In the summer of 1867 a frontier Kansas town on the east side of Mud Creek, a little place called Abilene, with a saloon, a one-room store, a six-room hotel, and a dozen log cabins, suddenly developed growing pains. By fall the Union Pacific had built a hundred-car railroad switch, and a man named Joseph Mc-Coy had built a shipping yard for a thousand head of cattle, a barn, an office, a livery stable, a bank, and a $15,000, three-story frame hotel that could sleep eighty and feed at least two hundred more. Abilene was about to become a cow town. For McCoy, who knew the livestock business from the ground up, had sold the idea of trailing Texas Longhorns to a Union Pacific railhead at the end of the Chisholm Trail.

To the punchers trailing the vast Longhorn herds up from Texas, the whole long route to Abilene was the Chisholm Trail. For them it began at the Rio Grande, ran by way of San Antonio, Austin, and Fort Worth to Red River Station, and from there cut across the Indian Territory, now Oklahoma, near the present towns of Duncan, Chickasha, El Reno, Pondcreek, and Medford, into Kansas and on up to Abilene. Actually, however, Jesse Chisholm's loaded wagons, hauling buffalo robes and trade goods between his trading posts on the North Canadian River and the Little Arkansas, had rutted the famous trail across the prairie only in the Indian Territory and in Kansas.

Half Scotch and half Indian like the enterprising Colbert brothers who operated the Chickasaw ferries and "stands" on the

81

Natchez Trace, Jesse Chisholm had followed his mother's Cherokee people to their new home in the West, eventually marrying a Creek girl and establishing himself as a successful trader. And in the Indian Territory white men and red agreed on one point at least: Jesse Chisholm was "a man with a straight tongue." His reputation for honest dealing kept him in demand as interpreter and guide and often even enabled him to rescue white captives he discovered among the tribes. Interestingly, too, at Fort Gibson in the Indian Territory, a sister of Jesse Chisholm's mother married another man who made Western history — Sam Houston, former governor of Tennessee, and later hero of the Battle of San Jacinto in the Texas struggle for independence and first president of the new Lone Star Republic.

Prophetically enough, Jesse Chisholm had trailed 250 head of cattle, along with his loaded wagons, over his new route in 1866, but he would have been as surprised as any man west of the Mississippi had he lived to see the tossing horns of the huge herds that began to follow his wagon tracks in 1868 and hear his name in the songs of their punchers.

> *I woke up one morning on the Old Chisholm Trail,*
> *Rope in my hand and a cow by the tail,*

and properly sung by a man on a trotting horse, so the Texans claimed, the "Chisholm Trail Song" could do just about anything, from putting "life into a footsore cowherd and a saddle-sore puncher" to "throwing several kinds of panic into a bunch of Mexican cow thieves and into Indians on the warpath!"

What effect it had on a Longhorn bull, however, is not on record. Perhaps nobody felt like testing it out, for, according to stockmen, the Longhorn bull was the meanest critter that ever went on four legs, and the longer he lived, the meaner he got. Apparently, even in a pleasant frame of mind, he swaggered around threatening destruction to everything in sight, and when annoyed, he made nothing of tackling half a dozen regiments. At least,

82

General Zachary Taylor's columns, on their way to one of their most brilliant victories against overwhelming odds, got themselves thoroughly routed by a Longhorn bull whose temper was carelessly ruffled by a trigger-fingered private with a couple of spare bullets in his gun. Certainly no one on foot ever felt easy trying to argue sense into a temperamental beast whose horns measured 3½ to 6 feet from tip to tip!

Texas cattle, in those days, were predominantly of Spanish breed, for the Conquistadores had stocked their ranches and missions, and the herds had multiplied. By 1770, for example, the Mission of Espiritu Santo near Goliad, Texas, owned 40,000 cattle, and the Mission of Rosario west of the San Antonio River, 30,000. Comanche and Apache raids took a heavy toll — as many as 22,000 in a single raid — but generally Indian depredations did more damage to owners than to cattle. Few buffalo eaters cared for the taste of beef, and the Indians, raiding primarily for horses, often drove off cattle without killing them, simply to make life harder for the Spaniards. Often, too, ranchers themselves had to leave their herds behind to fend as best they could when repeated Apache raids necessitated abandoning frontier holdings, and during both the Texas Revolution and the Civil War, as still more ranchmen left home to fight, other domestic cattle wandered off to join the older wild herds. In fact, at the end of the Civil War, about 5,000,-000 Longhorns were roaming the Texas plains, ready for the taking by any man with a rope, a branding iron, and nerve enough to use them.

As a breed they had been running wild for a hundred years or more, and they were tough enough to make St. Louis buyers reflect that they had seen "plenty of buffaloes that were a lot more civilized!" They had survived drought, blizzards, insects, wolves, and Comanche arrows. They were built for speed and they knew how to take care of themselves. But Texans, returning to an impoverished state after the Civil War, were ready to try branding anything with a hide on and begin recouping their livestock losses

Lurking lobo wolves and coyotes waited
to pounce on straying calves.

and rebuilding their cattle industry. Mavericks, unbranded animals, made up the bulk of the wild cattle brought back into ranch
herds, for though honest cattlemen did not cut out calves under a
year old if they followed branded cows, any unbranded calf who
had been weaned was fair game. Actually, until unbranded calves
grew scarce enough to make proof of original ownership easier,
mavericking was not regarded as a form of rustling. That term,
incidentally, came from the efforts of a new owner to round up the
strays from a herd a man named Maverick had sold him. Ranging
over the grasslands, his men claimed unbranded cattle as the
Mavericks they were looking for, and the name stuck to unbranded
and unclaimed animals.

Fortunately for the Lone Star State, no quarter ton of Longhorn could faze her cowboys as long as the Chisholm Trail flourished, and where the herds went, there went the punchers.
Come spring, and the papers in the towns along the route reported
that the Trail was swarming with cattle. In 1876 Captain Richard

King's twelve trail herds alone totaled 30,000 head of cattle, and with each of King's herds went a $100-a-month trail boss, a $30-a-month cook, and fifteen $25-a-month trail hands. That was a lot of beef and a lot of payroll for one "spread" to walk north in a season, yet in the total that punchers trailed that year, 321,928 head, the King herds were just a few more Longhorns for cowboys to point north.

Long, hard, sweaty hours in the saddle; sourdough biscuits and black coffee; lonely nights riding guard around a bedded herd; choking dust sifting through the bandanna over a puncher's nose; rattlesnakes in a bedroll; raiding Comanches and Kiowas; rustlers from both sides of the border; swollen rivers to swim, and quicksand to suck down a steer; cows bawling for water; thunder rumbling and a whole herd beginning to drift; steers snorting and pawing the earth, tossing their mighty horns; lobo wolves and coyotes howling; more thunder and a midnight stampede — that was the Chisholm Trail. No wonder a trail boss organized his herd and his outfit carefully, trying to get some of the wildness out of his Longhorns before he hit the road, choosing his punchers from the best men on the owner's spread, and his cow ponies for their intelligence.

But of all the dangers of the long drive, the stampede was the most dreaded. A shred of tobacco or a hailstone landing in a Longhorn's eye had him on his feet, trampling the tails of the steers around him, and the whole herd would be off like the wind. A puncher's sneeze, a strange smell, the snort of a horse, even a prairie chicken, have started herds on a rampage that kept an outfit busy all night and half the next day. Sometimes an obstreperous steer touched off stampede after stampede until he was finally spotted for the troublemaker and swapped off to the Indians or simply cut out and shot. Herds with the wind really up have actually stampeded eighteen times in a single night, and though in a minor stampede the punchers might round up their cattle only a few miles away, a bad one could last a week and take the Long-

85

horns several hundred miles off the trail. Then Indians or white rustlers got busy or the steers mixed in with a herd of buffalo, and that was the last of the lot of them. And after any big stampede, the outfit could call itself lucky that had no puncher to bury beside the Trail with his cowboy boots for his headstone. But many a stampede was averted and many a nervous Longhorn bedded safely down again by a crooning puncher on a cow pony. Something slow and mournful made the most satisfactory lullaby for a trail herd, and some trail bosses would not even hire a hand who could not sing. Up in Abilene Joseph McCoy claimed he sat on the top rail of his stockyard nights to sing to a penned herd when the Union Pacific train roared by so they wouldn't stampede clear through his fences!

By the time the trail outfits reached Abilene, however, they were in no mood to spend any more time crooning to Longhorns. They had hit town with a terrific thirst, and they were off to quench it as they "hurrahed" the main street, shooting knobs off all the doors in sight. Abilene obliged them. Saloons, dance halls, and gambling spots were open twenty-four hours a day. Pianos and brass bands went full blast. Professional criminals, attracted by the easy money of the big stockmen and cattle kings, swarmed into town, and in the cattle season Abilene had more cutthroats and desperadoes than it knew what to do with. When things finally got too bad for the citizens to take, the town fathers moved the worst of the floating population down to Hell's Half Acre and hired some lawmen. Two of them, Tom Smith, mounted on his famous horse Silverheels, and Wild Bill Hickok, even managed to bring Abilene to heel. As marshal, Wild Bill liked to wear a Prince Albert coat, checkered trousers, and a silk vest embroidered with flowers, but no one who had ever seen him shoot ten bullets into a fence post and make just one small hole felt much like riling him. A pair of gamblers who ran the Bull's Head Saloon tried to get Wes Hardin, the Texas killer, to make Marshal Hickok his forty-sixth victim, but Hardin wasn't having any.

86

"If Bill needs killin'," he drawled, "why don't you do it yourself?"

It was Hardin, too, who said he had seen a lot of fast towns in his day and Abilene beat them all. But, then, Wes Hardin had not seen Dodge — "queen of the cowtowns; the biggest, wildest, happiest, wickedest, little city on the continent!"

As Abilene cleaned house and quarantine against Texas cattle grew more extensive, the terminus of the Trail shifted to other towns, but of them all, Dodge City on the Arkansas, at the head of both the Chisholm Trail cutoff and the newer Western Cattle Trail, was the most famous and the most notorious. Dodge had been wild and woolly from the beginning, when it was only Buffalo City, the camp of the buffalo hunters, 5 miles from Fort Dodge on the Santa Fe Trail, and headquarters for the bullwhackers hauling freight to the camps, ranches, and forts within a radius of 200 miles. Then, in the summer of 1872, when the Santa Fe Railroad came in, the old camp became a town named Dodge City after the fort, and the stage was set for what the Kansas newspapers called "the rip-roaring burg of the West; as rough a community as ever flourished under any flag; where they called

> *That day lost whose low descending sun*
> *Saw no man killed or other mischief done!"*

And of all the graveyards in America, Dodge's Boot Hill is still the most famous. Twenty-five people out of a population of five hundred were killed during the first year of Buffalo City's existence, and rechristened Dodge continued to use the same Boot Hill for a number of years. In Dodge, people said, "A man could break all the ten commandments in one night, die with his boots on, and be buried on Boot Hill in the morning." Nowadays nobody lies on Boot Hill, but visitors still flock to see the fake graves in the old graveyard with the heads and boots of concrete sticking weirdly up out of the ground.

As a matter of fact, Dodge City was not noticeably different

A crooning puncher on a horse averted
many a stampede.

from Abilene, except that whatever Abilene had, Dodge had more
of, including tramps, deadbeats, gamblers, swindlers, train robbers,
horsethieves, and cattle rustlers, and in Dodge as long as they used
their bullets on each other, nobody minded especially. That went
for the Texas punchers, too. Not even the town marshals con-
sidered it much of a crime for one transient to shoot another. All
Dodge asked of its visitors was that they quit taking their cow
ponies into saloons and dance halls and that when they came north
of the Deadline at the railroad tracks, they check their guns at the
racks neatly provided in corrals, hotels, stores, saloons, and gambling spots. The mayor would bring in some famous gun-slinger
to enforce these ordinances, and a gang of cowboys would run him
out of town.

But no one ever ran out Marshal Wyatt Earp or his deputy Bat
Masterson, not even Clay Allison who headed over from Colorado
to cut Earp down. Allison had already killed the marshals in
Cimarron, New Mexico, and Las Animas, Colorado. Besides,
Dodge City knew him of old; a man who had disagreed with him
some years earlier was buried on Boot Hill. Marshal Earp did not
lose any sleep over Clay Allison, however, and when the killer

88

struck Dodge, the Marshal took time to finish shaving before he strolled down Front Street, shoved a gun against his ribs, and sent him back to Las Animas.

Both Wyatt Earp and Bat Masterson were professional gamblers, cool as oysters in an emergency. Bat was limping from a leg wound received in a killing when he went to work in Dodge, but Earp said, "Even as a cripple, he was a first-class peace officer. He patrolled Front Street with a walking stick for several weeks and used his cane to crack the heads of several wild men hunting trouble." Neither man made any attempt to interfere with the celebrations of teamsters, buffalo hunters, and cowmen coming into Dodge as long as they did their livelier celebrating south of the Deadline, but under Earp's regime, "hurrahing" stores, saloons, and gambling halls on Front Street meant a night in jail and a fine as sure as shooting. Eventually, of course, Wyatt Earp and Bat Masterson moved on; there were many frontier towns telegraphing to fighting marshals to come clean them up. But by the time Dodge City settled down to real respectability, the tempestuous herd-trailing days were done.

Like the rest of the great trails West, the Chisholm Trail had played its part in the opening of our lands beyond the mountain barrier and the mighty "Father of Waters," the Mississippi. Over it had trailed the most tremendous migration of livestock in history. Its mixed herds, walked on to Cheyenne, Ogallala, and northern points, had hastened the settlement of the ranges in Wyoming, Montana, Colorado, and both Dakotas. Its beef herds had spurred railroad construction and the development of refrigerator cars, speeded the growth of Kansas City, Chicago, Omaha, Wichita, and Fort Worth as centers of meat packing, and created a vast new export business for the United States. But for Americans today, the Chisholm Trail still means wide horizons and thundering hoofs and the punchers and their songs from the state "that grew from hide and horn."

90

About the Author and Artist

Edith Dorian knows a great deal about books and writing. Her special interest since childhood has been American history and Indians—two subjects about which she has almost limitless information.

Ever since her days at Smith College, she has been writing short stories, articles, and reviews, and for a number of years she taught literature at the New Jersey College for Women at Rutgers University and received her master's degree at Columbia University.

TRAILS WEST AND MEN WHO MADE THEM is her fourth junior book —her other three are HIGH WATER CARGO, ASK DR. CHRISTMAS, and NO MOON ON GRAVEYARD HEAD.

W. N. Wilson, who was born in the north of England, has also been a student of American history for a great many years. After he had made many tramping and sketching trips along the Atlantic and Pacific coasts, some of his paintings were published in a book called ALONG THE MAINE COAST.

A well-known nautical illustrator, he did the drawing for SHIPS THAT MADE U. S. HISTORY.

www.ingramcontent.com/pod-product-compliance
Lightning Source LLC
Chambersburg PA
CBHW081258040426
42452CB00014B/2557